# Against #shortermism

## A few lessons on the importance of a long-term corporate culture

*To my entire family, who provided the inspiration for all my work, including this book. Also, to the students involved in Young Investors Society. May the lessons from our program allow all of you to invest wisely, so that you too can dedicate more time to your loved ones.*

When I first began learning about investing, I thought it was all about numbers. I thought that whoever could come up with the best algorithm or build the best financial model would outperform the market and make billions of dollars.

But the longer that I have been in the asset management industry, the more I have come to learn that it is really all about people. While we may initially just see numbers on a piece of paper, when we look beyond the surface it is people that make the decisions of how to spend the money. It is people that decide the strategy. It is people that create the culture of a company. And in the end, it is people who decide whether to buy a company's product or not.

Throughout my investment career, I have noticed a trend: a company's culture oftentimes is a deciding factor of what makes it or breaks it for a company. Some companies have a "grow at any cost" culture, and, unfortunately, they end up growing at much too high of a cost, often through taking on too much debt or expanding beyond their core competency.

Some companies become so wrapped up in the quarterly earnings game that they lose track of the long-term picture and end up losing their market. This is what Claudio calls #shortermism. But there are also those exceptional companies with a phenomenal culture, and you can feel that every employee eats, drinks and breathes a united goal.

More often than not, companies with a strong culture experience tremendous success.

*Claudio's deep dive into the culture at companies like Starbucks and Google (now Alphabet) show why an exceptional company culture can lead to powerful results.*

In recent years there has been a growing amount of research in the financial industry to understand people better. From behavioral economics to investor phycology, this has been a field of recent considerable focus. In our quest to continually improve as investors and analysts, it has become clear that the next frontier is to better understand human behavior.

I believe Claudio's study of corporate culture is an important piece of the puzzle. Understanding the people behind the organization, why they do what they do and how we can improve human behavior is so critical. If we can understand the culture in the organization, it will be one of the biggest leading indicators on whether that company will succeed or not. Frankly, it is an essential part of analyzing a company but one that is often overlooked or skimmed over by most investors.

Speaking of people, Claudio Brocado is one of the most amazing people I have met in my life. I first was introduced to Claudio while attending investor conferences early in my career. Claudio was a 'rockstar' of the investment industry. Every room that he walked into he was greeted by corporate CEOs, Wall Street brokers, and other investors would immediately walk up to him and give him a hug and want to speak with him.

Claudio is intensely optimistic, profoundly intelligent, and unendingly kind and warm. He is one of the most exceptional people I have ever met. Warren Buffett said *"It's better to hang out with people better than you. Pick out associates whose behavior is better than yours and you'll drift in that direction."* I feel that my life has become better because of the time I've spent with Claudio and the things I've learned from him. In building a culture for Young Investors Society (YIS), I knew we needed to attract people of the caliber of Claudio to lead it.

**About Young Investors Society**

I founded Young Investors Society because we're all investors. While I may be a professional fund manager as my day job, I'm also an investor of my family's earnings each month. Every fireman, lawyer, doctor, entrepreneur, and school teacher in the world is an investor. The sad thing is that most people have no idea how to invest successfully. According to JumpStart, over 2/3 of high school kids fail a basic financial literacy test. Most adults don't fare much better. Can you save more than you make? And where do you invest your money? Those two questions determine all the wealth that you will earn in your life. There's hardly anything we can teach that is more important than that.

Young Investors Society (YIS) is a non-profit organization that was formed in 2014 with the intent of teaching high-school students how to answer these questions. YIS is quickly building a vibrant community of young investors from high schools around the world. We don't just learn about finance, we practice it. We don't just read about stocks, we analyze them. We don't just talk about the benefits of investing early, we set up a program (the "Dollar-a-Day Challenge") where students actually start investing real money and receive donor matches from sponsors that incentivize creating the habit early in life. The fun thing about investing is that anyone can do it, even starting with only a few bucks.

YIS has built a world-class curriculum to teach investments basics and fundamental stock analysis. There are so many gimmicks and get-rich-quick schemes out there regarding the stock market, but our goal is to teach the correct, time-proven, long-term investing principles in an engaging way. As the founder of YIS, it is my task to put together a dream team of investors and teachers to write the curriculum. Claudio has been one of the most prominent contributors to the curriculum of Young Investors Society. This book is an excellent extension to his investment wisdom.

A "Million Dollar Decision"

A while back, I was presenting to a group of students at a local public high-school. I showed a pretty standard slide that calculated how much money you would accumulate by the time you retire if you started investing at different ages. The assumptions were pretty basic. It assumed you invest $1,000 per year with a market return of 10% (the standard stock market return of the past 100 years). The chart went like this:

**Amount Saved by the time you retire** (at 65 years old, assuming $1k/yr at 10%)

- Starting at age 45 -> $71,638

- Starting at age 35 -> $211,885

- Starting at age 25 -> $593,064

- Starting at age 15 -> $1,629,074

I said "I hope you can see that starting young really makes a big difference." I was about ready to move on to the next slide, when a very bright girl sitting in the back raised her hand and said "Wait Mr. Fletcher, that can't really be true. That's a difference of a million dollars on that last one." I responded "Exactly! Your decision right now, today, as a 15-year-old whether to start investing is literally a million dollar decision. If you decide "Yes," and commit to it then you have literally just put over a million dollars in your retirement account. If you decide "No," I'll wait until after college to start investing, then you'll be like everyone else that scrimps and saves and probably can't retire when they would like." An audible gasp swept across the classroom. Ever since that day, I like to introduce the concept of investing early as the "Million Dollar Decision."

An Invitation to All Readers

I would invite every reader of this book to make a decision to start investing today. If you read this book and think to yourself "Well, that was interesting," but don't actually do anything with it, you are literally throwing away millions of dollars that should be yours over your lifetime. The younger you are when you read this, the bigger the opportunity.

If you're a high-school student, I would challenge you to open a custodial account with your parents and put a few dollars in your first stock or mutual fund. You can join Young Investors Society or start one up at your school to learn the valuable skills to navigate the stock market. If you're a parent or teacher, I would challenge you to consider a way to get involved and spread the word in your community to increase financial literacy. The best place to start making a difference is probably within your own family or within your classroom. I challenge you to build a culture of financial literacy in your community. Your efforts to invest today will pay powerful dividends that will impact not only your life, but lives for generations to come.

## Introduction

The financial world has evolved dramatically in the past few decades, let alone the last couple of centuries. Still, in recent years, much of the financial industry's evolution has not generally been well received by the public at large. Much of the financial innovation going back at least to the start of the millennium has focused on gaining scale, and much less on better serving the investing public, particularly the small retail investor.

In addition, increasingly complex and 'sophisticated' strategies, including those with esoteric derivative products, are at the core of the industry's innovation. The abuse of some of these complicated strategies was largely to blame for the global financial crisis late last decade.

The American public at large is less engaged with the financial industry than at any point in recent memory. There is growing talk of 'Main Street versus Wall Street'. The main ultimate reason for this, in my view, is that the culture of most of the well known financial firms has tended to emphasize short-term success. Leading politicians (not to mention Hollywood) continually use 'Wall Street' as a key scapegoat for the nation's problems, and increasingly talk about the need to 'break up the banks'.

I am as outraged as anybody else that no more individual executives ended up in prison as a result of their misdeeds leading up to the global financial crisis. There was not only incompetence, but also outright fraud surrounding the subprime mortgage crisis and all its many grave repercussions, including what I refer to as the global financial crisis (GFC), also known as the Great Recession.

Still, I am almost equally frustrated by the broad-stroke criticism of all of Wall Street. There were many individual 'bad apples' who should have been prosecuted. However, the apparently endless multibillion dollar fines that banks have been forced to pay in recent years are obviously not being paid by the individuals responsible. Rather, investors of all sizes are the ones who actually foot the large bill. If you have a pension fund, you likely are one of the millions of shareholders affected by the large bank fines.

Banks, as most large companies, are no longer owned by a handful of 'fat cats'. American corporations with listed stock tend to have very 'pulverized' ownership; what this means is that they are owned by many thousands of shareholders. When a small investor buys an exchange traded fund (ETF), let alone a more traditional equity mutual fund, he or she is buying a small share in a large number of companies, including most likely the big banks.

Throughout the world, there has been a trend in the last couple of decades towards the owners of capital doing better than the providers of labor; the gap between the 'haves' and the 'have nots' has generally grown on a global basis. This trend threatens to undermine progress towards continuing globalization and the spread of free-market capitalism around the world.

Even in the US, there are increasingly loud calls, particularly among young people, for curtailing the power of large companies. Legal suits including class actions against corporations all too often result in *all* shareholders having to shoulder the costs levied on companies due to misdeeds by a few corporate executives. Many US consumers do not realize that they are at the same time shareholders of firms they claim should be penalized.

That is why the 'us versus them' argument is of little practical relevance. There is no real, good long-term reason for the large chasm between Main Street and Wall Street. What is good for the stock market is good for the public at large, in the long run. It is true that many Americans do not own stocks, at least not directly. Still, as I have just noted, many more than probably realize it are indeed shareholders (of the banks and other large companies) through mutual funds, ETFs, pension funds, etc.

American public opinion, let alone justice, would have been better served if the individuals directly responsible for the abuses that contributed to the global financial crisis had been held personally liable. Nonetheless, many of them are probably no longer even employed at the large banks that continue to be held as scapegoats.

Thus, in my opinion, at this stage (at least in practical terms), the continuous cry against Wall

Street ends up amounting to more of a desire for revenge than for justice. Still, this does not mean I think most financial institutions are beyond reproach. What their critics probably have right is that a culture of 'short-termism' prevalent at many financial institutions, particularly some of the largest banks, did provide a fertile ground for the abuses perpetrated by a few.

Before we go further, a few additional clarifications are in order. What people mean when they refer to Wall Street tends to vary from person to person. Historically more linked to the actual geographic location of the New York Stock Exchange and many of the investment banks doing business there, the term is now used more broadly, to refer to the financial industry at large.

The line has blurred between traditional investment banks and commercial banking institutions, and this is probably at the core of what people still refer to when they talk about Wall Street. But some people use the term to refer to any type and size of financial firm.

Even among the banks, though, there were clear differences in how their key executives behaved at the time that led up to the global financial crisis. Banks such as Wells Fargo and JPMorgan Chase were asked by the US government for help in addressing some of the most pressing issues at the peak of the crisis. Both firms actually did not require any government financial support to survive the crisis. Still, in order to cooperate with the authorities (with the goal of reducing the stigma associated with a government bailout), they accepted troubled asset relief program (TARP) funds. This continues to be interpreted by the public at large as Wells Fargo and JPMorgan having also been 'bailed out' by the government.

Those TARP loans were subsequently paid in full by all major banks. Moreover, large financial institutions such as JPMorgan (JPM) were among the few private firms actually providing *any* financing at all at the peak of the GFC. According to chairman and CEO Jamie Dimon, JPM (and some of the large banks) were among the very few institutions rolling over loans as they were coming due at the height of the crisis. This provided necessary breathing room, particularly to small and medium-sized businesses.

I have come to very strongly believe that the single most important *negative* feature of the culture of many firms generically known as Wall Street is a pervasive short-term orientation. What I now call 'short-termism' is, in my opinion, the biggest enemy of everything many of us hold dear -- what I increasingly fear is holding the world economy back. Unfortunately, I fear it will be a formidable rival to combat as it is now well entrenched in our society. Technological advances of the last few decades have, in my view, helped to intensify the apparent need for immediate gratification. What it took meaningful time and effort to research in the past can now be accomplished through a quick Google search.

Then there's the US political system with what boils down to a two-year (very short term!) electoral cycle. There are presidential votes every four years, but 'mid-term' elections two years after each presidential vote, which means we're essentially always in election mode.

With the political landscape in constant flux, in an increasingly complex global economy, it is extremely difficult for the all-important business sector to plan and invest for the long run. The rules of the game keep changing (who knows what the next government will bring!). The tax code, let alone the overall regulatory environment, is nothing short of byzantine. It is chock-full of short-term fixes.

As Apple CEO Tim Cook recently said in a CNBC interview, with a dysfunctional government, companies have to take more responsibility. If government regulation does not provide more long-term certainty, we all have to fight short-termism (#shortermism) with whatever means we have at our disposal.

Companies such as Warren Buffett's Berkshire Hathaway (which, somewhat perversely, is classified as a financial firm), Apple (AAPL), Starbucks (SBUX), Alphabet (GOOGL), Amazon (AMZN) and Facebook (FB) are great examples of long-term thinking in action. As far as Berkshire Hathaway, given its conglomerate nature, it is not so much the corporate culture to which I refer. Here the importance lies in the corporate DNA of the individual subsidiaries. Warren Buffett makes cultural fit a key priority when making a major acquisition. He then lets each subsidiary's capable management continue to run the subsidiary in line with its existing long-term corporate culture. This is one of the reasons why the Oracle of Omaha never makes hostile acquisitions.

Another company that appears to have a favorable, long-term oriented culture, but that is not publicly traded, is Bloomberg. The global financial news and information giant has been able to successfully expand into an ever-larger number of media, propelled by what I believe to be an outstanding corporate culture.

Sometimes the need to focus on the long term means (or gives controlling shareholders the excuse for) adopting poor corporate governance practices, but the prescriptions against short-termism should be more creative than that. Michael Dell opted for taking his namesake company private. More (increasingly large) companies are choosing to stay private longer than ever. That cannot be the solution to the overall problem!

Using the #shortermism hashtag, I hope to contribute to a *long-term* discussion on ideas to combat our increasingly short-term oriented mentality in almost everything we do. Short-termism is what is creating an ever more complicated global environment for all of us to live and do business in. We all need to think of and work towards a better long-term future for our children, our children's children and many generations beyond.

As I will explain throughout this book, short-termism is a key *negative* cultural feature of many (though obviously not all) firms in the financial sector. Short-term thinking and stock recommendations seeking immediate gratification promote even more short-term corporate thinking. How can publicly traded companies plan for the long term?

In addition, one of the least well understood, yet important factors behind the growing divide between the financial industry and the investing public harkens back to the industry's drive to appear as if what it does is more akin to a science than an art. The financial industry, in the last couple of decades, has been hiring far more scientists than it used to in the past.

Financial innovation is, at least in the view of the public at large, more about esoteric strategies and high frequency trading than about catering to the evolving needs of the investment public. The personal touch has all but been lost. All the foregoing probably leaves the financial industry more vulnerable to disruption than it would like to be or than many other industries currently are.

I spent much of a career on a very specific sub-segment of the financial industry, active asset management, which itself has been disrupted in the last decade by the surge in interest in passive fund management (such as that used in ETFs). Within active fund management, my own experience was working on actively managed stock funds. Active fund management involves specific security selection. In the case of stock or equity funds, the managers evaluate individual companies to assemble a portfolio of stocks of publicly traded companies in order to create and manage an equity mutual fund. Within stock funds (as in many other areas of Wall Street), I believe the industry has been gravitating towards a more 'scientific' approach.

Thus, both the equity buy-side (the money-management side of the business – the buyers of stocks) and the sell-side (the investment bank side of the industry, where the specific equities are recommended) focus increasingly on the quantifiable metrics that make some stocks appear more attractive than others. The more scientific, the better...this makes you sound smart and gives you credibility! Still, Main Street does not seem to be buying it. Perhaps the attempt to sound smarter is linked to an unusual fact in the stock fund management business (the equity buy-side). A key message to investors by Warren Buffett is to pay close attention to management fees.

As Mr. Buffett explains, a unique feature of the stock investment businesses is that the 'professionals', in the aggregate, cannot do better than amateur investors. This is true in gross terms, let alone net of fees! The reason for this is that, in the aggregate, the relative performance of actively managed stock funds is essentially a zero-sum game. In other words, it is literally impossible for all equity fund managers to beat the index, which is how relative performance is measured. Yet, all active fund managers charge fees to manage their funds. Given that index funds, notably certain ETFs, charge much lower management fees than actively managed funds, it is no surprise investors have been switching to low-cost ETFs.

An area of finance that has traditionally received little attention, particularly in the public markets, is the understanding of corporate culture. The secular trend towards quantitative finance means that ever less attention is paid to such 'softer' issues. Yet, I increasingly believe that company culture is a key determinant of corporate success and (at least in the long run) stock price performance. Therefore, there is a meaningful opportunity to add value by assessing the strength and quality of a company's culture.

# SECTION ONE – TOP-DOWN FACTORS

## CHAPTER ONE

### A primer on the importance of corporate culture

The main focus of this book is this under-researched and under-appreciated factor in public stock research. As investment strategies become popular and tend to get crowded, their effectiveness tends to diminish. This is a function of the fact that, as I have explained based on Warren Buffett's assertions, actively managed stock funds in the aggregate represent a zero-sum game. True long-term investment that pays close attention to corporate culture is *not* a commonly utilized investment strategy these days. There is meaningful, long-term potential for adding value through more thoroughly assessing corporate culture as an integral part of the process of evaluating public equity investments.

Based on my experience, a company's culture tends to determine what management style succeeds in the specific company. In a sort of feedback loop, a company's culture helps to determine its management style, which in turn tends to influence the culture of the company and how it evolves over time. In a sort of self-selection process, a company's unique culture attracts like-minded individuals to join and stay there, leading to perpetuating that specific culture.

Interestingly, according to Ben Fletcher, an executive focusing on venture capital (VC) investments, culture is an area of key focus by investors at such early-stage companies. In Fletcher's words, for example, "Sequoia Capital is known for placing a huge premium on corporate culture as they invest." Fletcher adds: "as a VC investor, we place a lot of value on the team and the corporate culture because they are key indicators of how the company will do when it hits hard times (and whether or not they will be successful)." Thus, at some point between the VC stage and the public markets, culture as a factor in equity research arguably all but disappears.

I was fortunate to have had the opportunity over many years to interact with many different management teams from a wide range of industries and with a large variety of management styles. Evaluating how those different management styles have influenced over the years the quality of the companies' operations helped me to develop insights into what seems to work, where and why. There seems to be a direct link between management quality (and how well a particular management style fits a company's culture), the success of the company's operations, its financial results and the performance of its stock over the long term.

In this book we will focus on a few specific traits of corporate cultures and management styles that tend to result in operating success and strong long-term stock performance. When I evaluate a stock for long-term investment, one of the most important characteristics on which I focus is the company's culture or DNA. As I already hinted, I believe that culture is an attribute of a company that tends to change only very little over time, even from CEO to CEO. I think of the culture of a company as something akin to the character of a person. In other words, company culture is a relatively stable, resilient attribute, so I will use *DNA* as a synonym for *culture* throughout this book.

Still, I believe that when new management (or a management with a renewed commitment to changing a company's culture) focuses its efforts on improving this specific attribute, the results tend to be very meaningful to stock price performance in the intermediate to long term. Thus, contrary to DNA, which is a more fixed attribute, a corporate culture *can* be changed with substantial work.

So why do analysts and investors focus so little on corporate culture? My best guess is that a key reason for this is the difficulty of quantifying a company's culture and grading it as a stock attribute. The main ultimate purpose of this book is to develop a framework to assess corporate culture to aid the equity investment process.

***What I look for in terms of corporate DNA is at its best a purposeful, results-oriented, mission-driven culture that provides a supportive environment in which employees want to do great work aligned with the broader company mission, which is larger than the company itself.***

Just a few examples of large companies that have such a favorable culture would include Alphabet (previously known by the name of its largest division, Google), Starbucks, Apple, Anheuser-Busch InBev, Costco, Netflix and Nike. At the opposite end of the spectrum, unfortunately given that it is where I spent most of my business career, is the financial industry.

When I first started the research for this book, my working hypothesis was that *all* companies should strive to achieve the 'best' possible culture. Increasingly, however, I believe that perhaps even more important than a 'favorable' corporate culture per se, a stable, predictable and purposeful culture is key to long-term success.

Through the self-selection mechanism that is likely to be ingrained by a durable culture, as I explained earlier, individuals will be attracted to and likely to stay for the long run in a company with a *strong* culture. Thus, again, what really seems to matter most is *long-term* relative stability of the culture, and not necessarily its subjective quality.

What is a 'good' culture to some, may well seem like a terrible culture to others. Amazon (AMZN) is, in my opinion, a great company in many ways. Yet, I for one would not characterize AMZN's culture as 'great'. There has been meaningful controversy regarding this extremely successful company's corporate culture. Still, it is according to most accounts purposeful and mission-driven. Much of the criticism centers around the Amazon culture being too 'intense'. But in the words of founder and CEO Jeff Bezos according to an article on *The*

*Verge,* "we never claim that our approach is the right one — just that it's ours — and over the last two decades, we've collected a large group of like-minded people,...Folks who find our approach energizing and meaningful."

The financial services industry includes many firms with corporate cultures that are far less than ideal, but the 'problem' is particularly acute on the sell-side. This, undoubtedly, contributes to the very poor reputation the industry increasingly has among the American public. Interestingly, my theory is that the pervasive valuation discounts at which the stocks of financial firms trade are, at least to an extent, due to their lack of favorable cultures.

Finally, a company's culture is also somewhat akin to the issue of confidence. It is said that building confidence takes long, hard work, yet confidence can be lost very quickly. This is also the case with the reputations of both companies and individual persons. While difficult and time-consuming to build a good reputation, a bad one can be quickly 'earned'. Once a bad reputation has been established, it is extremely difficult to reverse and make out of it a good reputation.

Likewise, a good corporate culture takes a long time to evolve and get ingrained. It is easier for a bad leader to destroy a great culture than for a great leader to turn around a case of bad corporate culture. Thus, I believe that culture is less sticky on the upside (towards a better culture) than on the downside.

It is also worth noting that the more stable a favorable company culture, the easier it is for the relevant company to deal with disruptive change. A strong, purposeful culture can help a company better deal with an adverse external environment. Such a positive culture can also help a company be more flexible and more successfully reinvent its whole business offering than a company where the workforce is not as aligned with the corporate leadership.

The first example that comes to my mind is the aforementioned Amazon, but Netflix would be a close second. According to Netflix CEO Reed Hastings, the company's culture is not optimized for short-term efficiency. He has fostered a culture where some inefficiencies are allowed, even welcomed, in the short run, in order to make the company more agile in the long run. Netflix initially disrupted the DVD video rental market, then led by long-gone Blockbuster, with the introduction of DVD rentals through the Internet.

The original Netflix customers could order their DVDs online, and the goods were physically delivered to the customers' mailing address. Netflix's corporate culture enabled the company to then repeatedly change its business model into what it is today. In other words, short-term inefficiencies, in the Netflix way, make the company more resilient for the long run, which is what truly matters.

Another key feature I look for when selecting a long-term equity investment is a company's competitive advantage or economic moat, as

Warren Buffett has taught us. I strongly believe that a good management, supported by a strong corporate culture, can help not only maintain, but even expand and fortify a company' moat. Netflix did not have much of a sustainable competitive advantage when its main line of business was DVD rentals.

Now, increasingly strong in the creation and development of its own proprietary video content, Netflix has not only built itself an economic moat but is arguably constantly expanding it and fortifying it. In the words of author NassimNicholas Taleb, you would say Hastings has created an 'antifragile' culture at Netflix. Conversely, Blockbuster's culture arguably made the company fragile, and it eventually went bust.

*Is a misinterpretation of traditional value investing partly to blame for short-termism?*

As I have mentioned, I fear that short-term thinking has become increasingly pervasive. When it comes to buying stocks, I wonder if a misinterpretation of traditional value investing may be partly to blame. Valuation ratios such as P/BV (price to book value) and P/E (price to earnings) are rather static and almost by definition focused on short-term statistics, particularly in the case of the P/E ratio. The most readily available version of this metric is even backward looking (price to *trailing* earnings per share).

I believe that most investors generally underestimate the true value represented by less-tangible attributes, such as the all-important corporate culture. This is particularly stark in the case of companies with immense cash generating capabilities, which traditionally would be considered growth stocks. This is more likely to be the case at a time of profound disruption in a large number of industries. Therefore, my thesis is that investors generally define value way too narrowly.

Conventional valuation metrics essentially view earnings and cash flows as what they currently are or are *likely* to be and not as what a proactive management of a company with a strong corporate culture *should* be able to deliver. This immediately brings to my mind Alphabet, the company previously known as Google (still its key division and cash flow generator).

A key feature of the Alphabet corporate culture entails looking at issues as they *could* be, and not simply as they currently are or are likely to continue to be. Starbucks also comes to mind on this topic. Its CEO and long-time leader responsible for its unique corporate culture (Howard Schultz) writes in his book *Pour Your Heart Into It: How Starbucks built a company one cup at a time,* "I saw Starbucks not for what it was, but for what it could be."

In this book, I will discuss some topics (some of which would seem far afield from corporate culture), as *I would like them to be.* The contentious political debate as the 2016 presidential election year in the US continues to unfold highlights a few key issues. The surprising success during the primary season of 'anti-establishment' candidates in both parties, to a not negligible extent in my view, is due to the fact that government officials have not bothered to carefully explain to constituents the long-term virtues of free-market capitalism in general and free trade in particular.

As I have already discussed at some length, it is true that misdeeds by some players in a deregulated financial industry contributed to the global financial crisis. It is also true that a meaningful share of the population at large appears to be outraged by the fact that no 'fat cat' went to prison as a result. But I also believe that the financial industry as a whole has been even more discredited than it deserves to be.

The financial industry and the government could have done a much better job of educating the public. That is why this book features sections devoted to explaining some of the key functions of financial firms in the healthy functioning of the economy, as well as the important role of free trade in the world's economy.

More than trying to perform an in-depth analysis of these issues and focusing on what has gone wrong, my emphasis will be on what can be done better going forward. If I can sum it all up in one term it would be the *long term.* Moving away from instant gratification toward more of a long-term focus would go a long way towards solving the challenges that have made a surprisingly large share of the population move away from support of free trade in particular, but even free-market capitalism in general.

## CHAPTER TWO

### Free Trade improves the welfare of *all* countries adopting it, in the *long run*

Contrary to the ongoing political rhetoric, international trade is *not* a zero-sum game. *All* countries that adopt free trade tend to benefit in the long run. That, of course, does not mean that *everybody* benefits. As countries specialize in industries where they enjoy competitive and comparative advantages, these may thrive, just as other industries are likely to suffer or even disappear altogether.

Because of the geographical concentration of certain industries prior to the spread of free trade and globalization, there can be entire regions in a particular country, which see their economies devastated as a result of free trade. Governments should not only do a better job of explaining the broader benefits of free trade to their constituents.

Perhaps even more importantly, the 'establishment' can do a much better job of cushioning the negative impacts of globalization on the most affected regions and segments of society. Retraining of workers in the worst hit industries, as well as other social 'safety net' programs have not been sufficiently and effectively utilized to minimize the adverse impact from free trade on part of the population.

Long-term, sustainable productivity growth can only come from improvements in the educational systems of the affected regions. Much more investment in what I call intellectual infrastructure is desperately needed.

What most bothers me about the anti-free-trade (protectionist) rhetoric so common in this year's US presidential election primaries of both parties is that the candidates are *promising* to have manufacturing jobs return to the US. Implicitly threatening global trade wars, the rhetoric centers around the jobs that have moved away from the US to countries with lower labor costs.

An old cliché jokes that if jobs truly moved to the countries with the lowest labor costs, a country such as Bangladesh would be getting most of the gains in global employment. The implied criticism of such a simplistic assumption is quite valid. I strongly believe that the countries that are likely to perform best over the long term are those that manage well a gradual transition towards higher-value added sectors. The goal should never be for a country to have cheaper labor; instead, the long-term focus should be on *better,* more educated and productive qualified labor.

*The low-end manufacturing jobs that initially "moved" from the US to Mexico, to some extent as a result of the North American Free Trade Agreement (NAFTA), subsequently "went" to China as that country joined the World Trade Organization (WTO). China has recently been losing low-value-added jobs to countries such as Vietnam.*

*Low-value-added* manufacturing jobs will never return to the US; nor should they, in my opinion. To the extent that such production does make its way back to this country, it will be performed by robots, not by American workers lacking the necessary skills. Short-term oriented political moves such as *mandating* $15 an hour minimum wages in New York and California are likely to do more long-term harm than good.

*I strongly believe in the virtue of rising wages over time. However, such rising incomes cannot just be legislated.* Productivity growth facilitated by improving educational levels and long-term oriented corporate cultures will inevitably lead to growing employee compensation over the long haul, in my view.

The concerns about people not being able to make a 'living wage' on the currently-legislated minimum level, in the short run, should be handled through fiscal measures such as an expansion of the earned income tax credit in the US.

The US needs to focus on its competitive advantages for its own job growth. As capital follows economic value added, better paying jobs will be created in an American economy in which the workforce is better trained and thus more productive.

The US should focus its efforts on better educating the workers of the future information economy. America will not revisit what some call its 'best days' by trying to again become a global low-cost manufacturing economy. Even policy makers in countries such as India and China already understand this also applies to their own less-developed economies.

The US will remain the major hub for innovation and high technology, key ingredients of the information economy, for decades to come. This country is great (by many measures, greater than ever), and its best days lie still ahead, but it also has more to lose than to win from a global trade war. I remain optimistic that reason will prevail in the end.

In the meantime, free trade has come under attack during this presidential election year, and not only from the left. Still, as the Heritage Foundation states in a recent report on the subject, "free trade policies do not just promote economic growth, they encourage freedom—including protection of private property rights and the freedom of average people to buy what they think is best for their families, regardless of attempts by special-interest groups to restrict that freedom."

Contrary to what one would think given the surprising strength during the primary season of candidates denouncing free trade, the Heritage Foundation report states "most Americans are open to the idea of more free trade. According to a 2014 survey by the Chicago Council on Global Affairs, 65 percent of Americans believe that 'globalization, especially the increasing connections of our economy with others around the world, is mostly good for the United States.' A 2014 Pew research center survey found that 68 percent of Americans believe growing trade and business ties with other countries is 'a good thing.' A 2015 Pew survey found that 58 percent of Americans believe that trade agreements have been 'a good thing' for the United States.

Not surprisingly, when The Heritage Foundation's American Perceptions Initiative asked, 'Which is more important? Allowing free trade so companies can buy the inputs they need at a lower cost, low-income families can buy clothing at more affordable prices, and the economy can create new jobs, or allowing congress to protect some politically connected industries from low-priced imports,' just 9 percent of Americans chose protectionism."

Admittedly, the 'conservative' wording of the question probably led to the overwhelmingly favorable response towards free trade. More recent polls in the midst of the presidential primary season in the US do point towards more protectionist sentiment in the US, a country that has arguably led the spread of free trade around the world in recent decades. In addition, and worryingly, a majority of millennials reportedly do not believe in the free-market economic system, according to polls!

Former New York mayor and business and financial news tycoon Michael Bloomberg recently said that it is not globalization but technology that is the root cause for job destruction. He also emphasizes that the role of government should be to cushion the impact of those job losses. As I noted earlier, this is where the 'establishment' has failed, and we have seen the backlash in what amounts to popular votes against free trade.

Nonetheless, contrary to such popular perception, the US as a whole has not fared poorly in a world of freer international trade. According to Warren Buffett, in 1970 exports were 5% of US GDP vs. 12% (of a much larger GDP now). The US has yet more to gain going forward from the spread of free trade around the world.

Unfortunately, there is much misunderstanding (and perhaps even deliberate misinformation) regarding how the Chinese currency has *actually* behaved in the last couple of decades! China has admittedly been able to garner an outsized share of the market for imports in the US. This, however, has been propelled by the country's entry into the WTO, and not by a deliberate policy of 'currency manipulation'. Please consider the following facts. When the Chinese yuan or RMB, as it is also known, was actually devalued in 1994, it had an 8 'handle'. In other words, it took more than 8 RMB to buy one US dollar.

It has *appreciated* in the last couple of decades to about 6.5 to the dollar. It takes *fewer* RMB (roughly 6.5 versus more than 8) to buy one US dollar, which means that the Chinese currency has *gained* in value, even when compared to a relatively strong US currency in world markets.

In August 2015, there was much press coverage of another Chinese RMB devaluation having taken place. Still, this was a minor adjustment that did not amount to more than 5% against the US dollar, as the Chinese government actually changed the currency 'basket' it uses for what it calls the daily currency 'fixing'. In the meantime, the Mexican peso, which devalued from a 3 handle in 1994, hovers around 18 today! This gives you an idea of the magnitude of the **revaluation** the yuan has experienced relative to the currency of the other major 'emerging markets' trading partner of the US.

While I am by no means an expert on the Chinese economy, I do know the Mexican corporate sector, as well as the country's monetary, fiscal and currency policies quite well. Therefore, I can confidently attest to the fact that there is no deliberate manipulation of the Mexican peso to weaken it against any other currency.

The fact that the Mexican currency has indeed *devalued* meaningfully against the US dollar, let alone the Chinese RMB, in the last couple of decades has not been a development welcome by most Mexican citizens and/or institutions. It is almost an issue of national shame to have such a weak currency.

What this does demonstrate, however, is that countries are really not in charge of the relative value of their currency when compared to those of countries with stronger economies, particularly when the countries in question have relatively open trade policies and their currencies float increasingly freely.

Getting back to the *Middle Kingdom*, the Chinese are actually trying to 'depeg' the RMB from the USD. The International Monetary Fund (IMF -- and indeed also the US) wants China to have a more freely floating currency that truly belongs in the special drawing rights (SDR) basket to which it was recently added. In fact, the Chinese RMB inclusion in the IMF's SDR basket was a key milestone in the march of the Chinese economy towards global recognition as a major market economy.

I am a firm believer in the net long-term benefits of global free trade. Therefore, I cannot join the growing chorus advocating new trade barriers and abrogation of trade treaties. As is often the case in other areas, rather than more rules and regulations, what we truly need is better enforcement of already *existing* rules.

I do empathize with calls for the need to have a more level playing field through strict enforcement of rules embedded in free-trade agreements. In fact, that is already happening. Chinese imports of cold-rolled steel have been recently slapped a nearly 266% anti-dumping tariff. Freer access to the Chinese market for US firms does seem generally like a fair demand.

# CHAPTER THREE

## Finance is an essential component of a growing economy

Even the harshest critics of the financial industry as it now exists in the US must understand that, at the very least, finance is a 'necessary evil' for the adequate functioning of the global economy. That said, the financial industry is ripe for disruption due to both technological advances and the poor reputation from which it suffers. The industry's bad reputation, as I have mentioned, is due in large part to the short-term orientation that has characterized many of the corporate cultures of firms in the sector.

Like trade, financial services evolved over the centuries of human development to make the workings of the global economy ever more efficient. Going briefly back to trade, it all started when, after the hunting and gathering stage, humans began to form settlements and cultivate the land. The early agrarian societies first started very local trade through a barter system whereby people would begin to specialize in what they could do or produce. Those early traders would offer their goods or services in exchange for those they themselves needed but lacked.

This budding specialization gradually led to efficiencies as individuals focused on what they were good at. The early barter system subsequently evolved into the use of currency to pay for goods and services. Fast forward a couple of millennia, and now *countries* focus on their own competitive advantages to more efficiently participate in the increasingly global economy.

The use of currency was arguably the first step in the evolution of financial services. The creation of credit and the fractional reserve banking system were key mileposts in the development of the financial industry. It would be impossible to imagine a modern economy without the aid of financial services. In fact, the more developed a country's financial system, the richer the country as a whole tends to be.

This is not to say that there are no problems with today's financial industry. In fact, as I note extensively throughout this book, the financial industry unfortunately displays one of the worst cases of dysfunctional corporate cultures. This makes the modern financial industry vulnerable to disruption by arguably more enlightened, nimble new players. Still, the remainder of this chapter will focus largely on the virtues of modern finance.

Credit is an essential component of a well functioning economy. It enables economic activity that would otherwise not take place. It helps to recycle the savings of economic participants into investment for the growth of the economy.

A recent comment in *Barron's,* the weekly financial publication, makes the point more succinctly than I ever could. Martin Conrad, "celebrating the Wealth of Nations" (referring to the 240th anniversary of the publication of Adam Smith's *An Inquiry Into the Nature and Causes of Wealth of Nations,* writes "investment and extensive markets were necessary to unlock the wealth-generating power of that labor force. Agriculture provides the early model. A farmer tills, plants, tends his crop, then harvests and sells it, which is when he finally gets paid. But what does the farmer live on before he sells his crop?

Unless a farmer is financed by his own savings or someone else's, there will be no crop, no new wealth, no work, for he must have money for him and his family to live on while he produces what he and others will consume.

This is the crucial role of investment; it makes productive work over long periods possible. Smith saw that investment was also 'consumption at almost the same time by a different set of people'. The same money invested in a farmer's production is also spent as consumption for a farmer and his family."

The temporary freezing up of credit at the height of the global financial crisis gave us all a sneak preview of what would happen in a world without credit. Furthermore, try to imagine having to come up with the entire amount of cash to buy your first home without any mortgage.

Governments, despite their ability to create currency at the sovereign level, undoubtedly also need access to credit to function and provide necessary public services. Corporations too, even those with net cash, require credit to facilitate their operations, if nothing else to smooth out timing differences between revenues, expenses and investments.

As companies start to grow beyond small entrepreneurial ventures, they need credit to finance their development. In modern financial systems such as that of the US, equity financing replaces or more likely complements credit to foster the growth of companies.

Financial firms, loosely known by the general public as Wall Street, help facilitate the process of getting companies of all sizes the funds they need to operate smoothly and grow well into the future. From commercial banks providing working capital and trade finance loans to fund exports, to investment banks underwriting equity offerings; from insurance companies helping individuals and corporations deal with risks, to asset managers that help people reach their financial goals, such as a worry-free retirement; financial companies satisfy important needs in a complex economic system.

I would argue that the poor reputation of the financial industry is also partly due to the lack of more meaningful public relations efforts by industry participants. Large banks, in particular, as I have noted, have become the scapegoats of substantial political rhetoric, and rather than defend themselves in the court of public opinion, they have apparently instead chosen to just lay low and take the pain.

Just like governments (both led by Democratic and Republican administrations) have failed to explain the benefits of free trade to the population at large, the financial industry has not bothered to try to justify its existence to the public. As I previously noted, the government could and should do a substantially better job of cushioning the negative consequences to the most affected segments, let alone explain the net benefits of free trade to the nation as a whole.

Robert Dilenschneider of the Dilenschneider Group publishes an always thought-provoking report on the state of the world; he has recently been vocal about the need for better public relations (PR) efforts on the part of the financial industry. Following are excerpts from a report published by the Dilenschneider Group in January 2016.

"One of U.S. regulators' central goals in the wake of the global financial crisis was to reduce risk-taking among banks holding federally insured deposits. There is no doubt they have been successful. Across a variety of financial markets and businesses, banks have downsized operations or, in many cases, exited entirely. But even the best intentions come with consequences. In 2016, markets may well discover whether this logical effort to limit risky behavior among banks has achieved the broader goal of making the financial system safer and more stable, or if it has created a new and dangerous set of systemic risks.

As new regulations reshape the market, activities abandoned by heavily regulated banks are not going away. Rather, they are simply moving to businesses and venues that are less regulated and more difficult to monitor. For example, non-bank lenders— businesses that provide credit without funding themselves with deposits—are capturing a growing share of business in mortgages, commercial real estate, small business/middle-market banking and other key areas of the U.S. economy. Included in this group are a broad mix of online lending platforms, private equity firms, business development companies, investment funds and others." In other words, the critics of Wall Street should be careful what they wish for. Just calling for 'breaking up the banks' may well create more problems than it solves.

Finally, the 'too big to fail' banks are arguably already excessively regulated. Rules and regulations implemented since the GFC subject them to a long list of requirements, including having to get official authorization from the Fed before setting their upcoming shareholder remuneration (dividend and stock repurchase) programs each year.

## **Demographic, social and political factors converge to highlight the need for better corporate cultures**

I have always believed there is no better way to conservatively build great wealth over the long term than the stock market. Yet, Wall Street and anything related to it seem to be so discredited that today's youth is not inspired to get involved in equities at all.

To some extent, as I have argued above, the global financial crisis probably helped give the financial industry generally a much worse reputation than it deserves. Before joining the financial sector, I worked for eight years in the restaurant industry. I can honestly say that, based on my own experience (as a share of its own workforce), the financial industry has at least as many wonderful people as any in the service sector.

As I have repeatedly stated, what ails the financial industry, is a case of poor corporate culture. But this can be addressed, and I believe, sooner or later it will. In the meantime, more engagement between Wall Street and millennials is required.

The so-called millennial generation does seem generally less open to equity investing than previous generations were at the time they were in the age range of millennials today. Having seen their parents go through the burst of the TMT (technology, media and telecommunications) bubble and the global financial crisis may have traumatized millennials enough to generally shun investing in publicly traded equities, at least for the time being.

As I have discussed, the current political environment, particularly the inflammatory rhetoric that characterized the 2016 primaries in both parties, chose Wall Street as a key villain. This does little to endear the financial industry to the people. At the same time, free-market capitalism more broadly seems to be under heavier attack than at any time in recent US history.

It is perverse, as I have implied, given that more people of average means own stocks (at least indirectly) than they realize. Thus, we already do have more of a shareholder democratic capitalism than many people appear to understand. Much additional progress is required along this front, however. A closer alignment between consumers and the companies from which they are customers is needed.

An important step in this direction could come from an idea such as the consume-to-invest stock ownership process for which I have filed a patent. If consumers are (knowingly) at the same time owners of the corporation from which they consume, this better alignment of interests will boost reciprocal loyalty, in my view.

The way forward is clearly not to dismantle the institutions that have brought us global progress, globalization, and have pulled tens of millions of people out of poverty in the developing world. In the long run, the interests of the average American are very much aligned with the continuing spread of free-market capitalism around the world. A richer emerging markets consumer will continue to demand the output of American innovation at ever-faster rates.

Again, this is not to say that the status quo cannot be improved. Indeed, one of the premises of this book is that we are at a crossroads of which a better, more sustainable form of free-market capitalism may emerge, and that all major stakeholders should work towards that goal.

Publicly traded corporations have a key role to play in the development of a more socially conscious shareholder democratic capitalism. Some companies, such as Starbucks, are already living by these principles, thanks to their unique corporate cultures. This book will attempt to establish a framework for assessing the quality of a company's culture. For the sake of simplicity, I will use the names Alphabet and Google rather interchangeably throughout the remainder of the book. The next chapter focuses on this great company.

# SECTION TWO – BOTTOM-UP EXAMPLES

## CHAPTER FOUR

### The Alphabet Example - Introduction

One of the most successful companies of our time (and arguably of all time) is indeed Alphabet. On February 2, 2016, the company broke yet another key record. Surpassing $500 billion in market value, Alphabet (GOOGL) became the youngest company ever to reach the very top of the world in terms of stock market value.

On that day, Alphabet for the first time surpassed Apple as the globe's largest company by stock market capitalization. How did GOOGL accomplish such a feat? It was not likely anywhere close to the top priorities of its young founders when they started the company.

Yet, the corporate culture that Larry Page and Sergey Brin imprinted on their company did create the DNA that the corporation needed in order to break such record of rapid value creation. By focusing on the very long term, Alphabet's founders created a winning culture that enabled the company to reach the global pinnacle of equity value in a record short time!

Alphabet itself attributes much of its success to its very unique culture. In their book *How Google Works,* Executive Chairman and ex-CEO Eric Schmidt and former SVP of Products Jonathan Rosenberg articulate in great detail and through numerous examples Alphabet's exceptional culture.

Schmidt and Rosenberg acknowledge that, given the company's relative youth, it has been somewhat easier to establish such a culture than it would be for a more traditional old corporation to dramatically improve its own. Still, the authors of *How Google Works* provide extensive and actionable advice for corporate managers anywhere trying to improve their own company's culture.

In my opinion, having read *How Google Works* and head of Alphabet's people operations Laszlo Bock's *WORK RULES!,* as well as the letter from the founders which became an integral part of the company's initial public offering (IPO) prospectus, Alphabet's corporate culture features a set of key attributes, which I will discuss later in this chapter and elsewhere in this book.

In the words of the two cofounders, they "have emphasized an atmosphere of creativity and challenge." This unique culture strives to attract the world's best "smart creatives" in the jargon of Schmidt and Rosenberg.

Alphabet cofounders Page and Brin termed their letter, which formed part of the Google IPO prospectus "an owner's manual" for Google shareholders. They did so, according to their own statement, "inspired by Warren Buffett's essays in his annual reports and his 'An Owner's Manual' to Berkshire Hathaway shareholders."

The Alphabet cofounders, like the Oracle of Omaha, stress strongly their focus on the long haul. In fact, they explain their use of a dual-class corporate structure at the time of the IPO as a key tool in achieving their major objective of being able to maintain their sharp focus on the long term. The following excerpt from their letter clearly emphasizes their commitment to the long haul.

*"As a private company, we have concentrated on the long term, and this has served us well. As a public company, we will do the same. In our opinion, outside pressures too often tempt companies to sacrifice long term opportunities to meet quarterly market expectations. Sometimes this pressure has caused companies to manipulate financial results in order to 'make their quarter.' In Warren Buffett's words, 'We won't "smooth" quarterly or annual results. If earnings figures are lumpy when they reach headquarters, they will be lumpy when they reach you'."*

Further emphasizing this point (and explaining why they can create more value in the long run than the more typical short-term focused corporations), Page and Brin state "Many companies are under pressure to keep their earnings in line with analysts' forecasts. Therefore, they often accept smaller, predictable earnings rather than larger and less predictable returns. Sergey and I feel this is harmful, and we intend to steer in the opposite direction."

Alphabet's cofounders repeatedly state their strong belief that their focus will result in higher profitability over the long run, albeit with the likelihood of more short-term volatility of results.

Some of the key elements of the Alphabet culture include an almost obsessive focus on the user. The company's workforce of 'smart creatives' is 'uniquely empowered' to 'launch and iterate' innovative products and to take risks. The company culture also includes the unique feature of "20 percent time," which enables (or rather, encourages) employees to use some 20% of their time to tasks outside their direct responsibilities. This is credited with some of Alphabet's most innovative ideas, and it encourages risk taking – not being afraid of failure. The following is a quote from *How Google Works.*

"The most valuable result of 20 percent time isn't the products and features that get created, it's the things that people learn when they try something new. Most 20 percent projects require people to practice or develop skills outside of those they use on a day-to-day basis, often collaborating with colleagues they don't regularly work with. Even if these projects rarely yield some new, wow innovation, they always yield smarter smart creatives."

More to the point of allowing for (and perhaps even profiting from) failure, the *How Google Works* authors say "To innovate, you must learn to fail well. Learn from your mistakes: Any failed project should yield valuable technical, user, and market insights that can help inform the next effort." They then proceed to paraphrase cofounder Page, "As Larry says, if you are thinking big enough it is very hard to fail completely. There is usually something very valuable left over. And don't stigmatize the team that failed: Make sure they land good internal jobs. The next innovators will be watching to see if the failed team is punished. Their failure shouldn't be celebrated, but it is a badge of honor of sorts. At least they tried."

This brings us to another key feature of the Alphabet culture that Larry Page is known for emphasizing...thinking big, going for "moonshots." But all this would not make Alphabet the great company it is if it were not an ingrained, *authentic* part of its culture. As Schmidt and Rosenberg put it, "We open by discussing how to attract the best smart creatives, which starts with culture, because culture and success go hand in hand, and if you don't believe your own slogans you won't get very far." Most (particularly large, public) corporations have a mission statement that espouses a certain culture.

Contrary to what is the case at Google, the overwhelming majority of corporate mission statements are only that; slogans most employees would not really know much about (and many of those who did know the mission statement would likely not agree that the company really lives by it). A company's culture, its true DNA, is what the company really practices day in and day out.

Therefore, Alphabet devotes substantial time and effort to what Schmidt and Rosenberg call one of the most important tasks of any employee, hiring. They can afford to be incredibly selective, and a core part of the culture is to "always hire people who are smarter than you are."

I believe the two most important attributes of the Alphabet corporate culture are its long-term orientation and its focus on the user (which are, in my opinion, mutually *inclusive*). This stands in sharp contrast to what the financial industry in the US tends to emphasize; for most financial institutions in this country it seems as if the sharpest focus is still on short-term profitability. Wall Street then increasingly demands from publicly traded corporations that they deliver the strongest possible *quarterly* earnings.

Analyst estimates and their stock recommendations live and die by the 'all important' quarterly results. Most publicly traded corporations in the US thus provide quarterly guidance, which is sometimes updated even more than once a quarter!

Again in the words of Alphabet's cofounders, "*In our opinion, outside pressures too often tempt companies to sacrifice long term opportunities to meet quarterly market expectations.*" Such pressures almost invariably come from Wall Street, very broadly defined to include everything from mutual funds to shareholder activist investors.

# CHAPTER FIVE

## The financial industry exacerbates the focus on short-term profits

Perhaps exacerbated by cultural traits that tend to encourage instant gratification and the very 'latest and greatest', the ethos of 'what have you done for me lately?' has increasingly taken hold on Wall Street. A popular saying in the financial industry states that 'you're only as good as your last trade!' Financial market participants seem ever more obsessed with the daily swings of the equity indices.

Stocks are favored or fall out of favor based on the company's latest quarterly earnings. Whether a stock 'is working' depends on how it has traded in the last few days. How can this encourage long-term thinking?

Additionally, it seems as if many market pundits think that, in order to impress the general public, they must sound smart, scientific and skeptical. Still, when it comes to long-term investing in the stock market, if you are *not* optimistic, the odds are actually stacked *against* you. The stock market is *not* the casino that many would have you believe. It really *all* is (and that is the *only* way to create great wealth) about the *long term.*

See in the equity market (particularly in a broad, deep bourse such as that of the US, let alone the aggregate *global* equity market), it pays to be optimistic in the long run. Equities are indeed the best, most secure investment path to *long-term* wealth – long have been and always will be. Again, the key is a true long-term orientation. One of the key reasons for this is that a well-diversified portfolio of global leaders will, in the aggregate, have the pricing power to pass on inflation to their customers, and then some.

In addition, I also have the following hypothesis. The news media, to attract eyeballs, has a permanent pessimistic bias. Bad, scary news always sold newspapers, got audiences for radio and TV newscasts and now generates click-throughs online. Thus, long-term equity investing gives us sort of a 'time arbitrage opportunity'.

In the long run, there will be more negative than positive news headlines. A dollar-cost averaging approach to long-term stock investing (in a global equity marketplace where the long-term trend is up, but punctuated by periodic sell-offs, often triggered by such negative news) is the best path to invest for wealth creation.

The dollar cost averaging method simply entails investing the same amount of currency on a periodic basis (say monthly) in the same stock or basket of stocks (say a well-diversified global equity ETF). This approach enables the investor to buy more shares when they are down in price, fewer when they are up, optimizing the investor's average cost basis.

Investors such as Legg Mason Miller's Bill Miller and Credit Suisse strategist Michael Mauboussin have also talked about time horizon arbitrage (THA). It allows investors with longer time horizons to profit from the investment opportunities created by #shortermism.

What I found through my years on the buy-side of the investment business was that the investment horizon has generally become increasingly short term, despite the rhetoric to the contrary. Since there are no absolutes, nothing works at the extreme. One can ride the stock of a company going into bankruptcy all the way down to zero under the illusion that one just has a longer time horizon than most investors. In other words, one should be careful not to try to hide investment mistakes (from oneself too) behind the excuse of having a long-term focus.

Nevertheless, in well-researched, sound investments, the long-term investor does generally have time on his or her side. Because investors tend to have very different time horizons and markets do trend up over time, the investor who can hold out longer term will tend to outperform, everything else being equal. All too often, investors bail out too early just because they did not give management enough time to execute on a successful strategy.

Therefore, the better the understanding an investor has of what a management strategy is and how long it will take to deliver on it, the better the chance of success with that investment. In some of the more extreme cases, a company that seems to be investing too much in the short term (thus rendering it *currently* less profitable than it otherwise would be), may actually represent a value stock if judged with a sufficiently long time horizon.

Yet, Wall Street seems to encourage investors to be traders (to have a short-term investment horizon). This, needless to say, has a positive impact on the financial firm's own short-term results by generating trading commissions, even if it may not serve the firm's, let alone the investor's best interests in the long run.

This is precisely the type of short-term thinking that the Alphabet cofounders emphasized worrying about in their letter to shareholders as the company was about to go public as Google (GOOG). Their company was not to provide guidance to Wall Street, and would retain its key cultural trait of long-term orientation.

It was perhaps this very candor that gained them a 'free pass' from the financial markets, and the company has continued to focus on the long term. Unfortunately, this is increasingly the exception that proves the rule for publicly traded companies and the demands that Wall Street tends to place on them. In fact, I even resorted to argue that the daily liquidity of publicly traded stocks was resulting in a sort of liquidity discount or 'liquidity curse.'

*Is the liquidity premium turning into a discount, and will this last?*

Historically, market participants have been willing to pay a premium for liquidity. In the equity market, in the hypothetical situation of two otherwise identical stocks, the one with the better trading liquidity would be expected to command a premium over the less liquid stock. In other words, everything else being equal, a stock that is easier to trade (one with better liquidity, i.e., more trading volume) would be expected to be awarded a higher valuation multiple than the less liquid alternative.

Warren Buffett has repeatedly noted how perverse it is that investors treat stocks so differently from real estate as an investment, simply because stocks are a much more liquid investment.

Paraphrasing Mr. Buffett, he once remarked how absurd it would be if a homeowner liquidated his or her home just because a neighboring home was sold at a discount versus its fair value. Homeowners do not track the theoretical value of their homes on a daily basis, and their investment psychology is not affected by the price fluctuations in their homes anywhere near to the extent that they are when they see the price swings in their stock holdings.

Therefore, Mr. Buffett often reminds us that his own mentor Benjamin Graham stated that, in the short term, the equity market functions as a voting machine, whereas in the long run, it is more like a weighing machine. That is one of the key reasons behind the success of *long-term* equity investing.

In the long run, the stock market weighs the cash generating ability of the underlying equities, whereas in the short term, fads and popularity tend to determine the price at which a particular stock trades at specific point in time. The implied discrepancy is what often creates wonderful buying opportunities in very desirable equities for the long term.

Yet another way to make this point is the following. The shorter the time horizon in the stock market, the more it resembles gambling. The instant gratification of 'day trading' is (even in terms neuroscience) not that different from casino gambling or even the thrill of video games. On the other hand, true long-term investing is like owning a company. That is really what long-term stock ownership means. The fact that stocks provide the *opportunity* of daily liquidity is only the icing on the cake.

How could trading liquidity ever be a bad thing? In the *short run*, better stock liquidity can certainly work against a stock price. Particularly in severe market-wide corrections (or if a specific stock is heavily owned by leveraged traders), a liquid stock may suffer disproportionally in the short term as traders take advantage of the relatively high liquidity to raise cash. This is when particularly attractive entry points are often created for long-term investors, but also why I advocate that such investors *never* use margin debt to increase their exposure to stocks.

Owning stocks on a leveraged basis exposes market participants to a sort of 'liquidity curse'. One may receive a margin call and be forced to liquidate a particular stock in a sudden market correction. But other than that, trading liquidity should always be considered a positive characteristic in a stock, in my view.

Still, and perhaps because investors seem to be increasingly shunning volatility, it appears almost as if the historical liquidity premium may be turning into a discount, and that the liquidity curse may be becoming more widespread and more of a permanent feature across equities!

As I have noted, millennials generally are much less engaged in public equity investing than prior generations were at their age. That said, investing in private equity seems much more popular of late. This is reflected both in the staggering valuations now prevalent in a number of late-stage venture investments, as well as in the growing popularity of 'crowdfunding'.

More investors than in the past, perhaps bolstered by young people including millennials, seem to be increasingly comfortable tying up their funds in illiquid investments. Equity is equity, and that which is *not* traded in the public markets is almost by definition riskier than publicly traded stocks, even with everything else being equal.

Therefore, it would seem as if more people are choosing venture capital and private equity at the expense of the public markets, at least implicitly preferring trading *illiquidity*. One hypothesis (other than Wall Street's poor reputation) that I have for this phenomenon is that it is less traumatic for those investors *not* to know exactly how much a particular equity investment they own is worth at a particular point in time, just as is the case in real estate.

Michael Dell was one of my early heroes as I started investing in technology stocks in the early 1990s. He penned an op-ed for *The Wall Street Journal*, which is now also a LinkedIn post of his. Personally, I was disappointed when Michael Dell succeeded in taking his company private. I had stuck with his stock through thick and thin.

As I explained earlier, 'time horizon arbitrage' allows long-term investors to actually profit from short-term thinking in the financial markets. This process, however, is short-circuited when controlling shareholders do not let minority shareholders stick it out through the hard times by taking companies private (or selling out) at cyclical lows.

Nonetheless, it is difficult to argue with Michael Dell's rationale as laid out in his post. Here is an excerpt of his comments. "Yet we find ourselves in a world increasingly afflicted with myopia—governments that can't see beyond the next election, an education system that can't see beyond the next round of standardized tests, and public financial markets that can't see beyond the next trade. This was what Dell faced as a public company. Shareholders increasingly demanded short-term results to drive returns; innovation and investment too often suffered as a result. Shareholder and customer interests decoupled."

Perhaps one of the key reasons for the emergence (and apparent steady increase) of what I call the perverse liquidity discount is that a growing number of investors is now favoring the relative secrecy of the private markets. Companies not in the public eye, as Dell notes, are freer to invest for the long run. This, again was the key fear highlighted by the Google cofounders, as previously noted. Few companies in the public markets are afforded that luxury, and the Alphabet team has arguably earned that right through hard work, candid statements and, most importantly, the strength of their corporate culture.

I am a strong believer in long-term investing, and hopefully, the liquid public equity financial markets will continue to generally enable long-term investors like me to engage in time horizon arbitrage. But sound corporate governance is also a key ingredient in attractive investments, in my opinion, and an important subcomponent of corporate culture more broadly. Corporate governance is also an area of focus for some activist investors, which brings us to another area worth discussing.

Just like Wall Street tends to be an aggregate term for anything having to do with the financial industry in the understanding of the average observer, all activist shareholders tend to be painted with the same brush by the layperson. The truth is that culture does vary broadly from one financial company to another, just like activist investors can be short or long-term oriented, depending on their individual investment philosophy.

Unfortunately, all too often all activist shareholders are feared by many market participants and company managements, even if some of them may bring more of a long-term view and welcome constructive recommendations aimed at improving a target company's culture.

Shareholder activism is often accompanied (and by some even equated) with calls for company managements to boost their shareholder remuneration programs, often with strong demands that corporate managements execute large stock buybacks. I do empathize with those who criticize share repurchases financed with significantly net-debt-boosting bond issuance as mere *financial engineering.*

Nevertheless, not all share repurchase programs are created equal either. Those that represent a prudent portion of a balanced shareholder remuneration program, which also includes a regular dividend policy, can constitute excellent financial *management* practice. Investors who hold on to their shares (or even better, reinvest the dividends on top of that) will see their stake in the company grow (accrete) over time as the float shrinks in corporations with stock buyback programs.

I do agree with those shareholder activists who claim there is a lot of progress yet to be made in advancing the cause of better corporate governance in the US, let alone the world. Improving corporate governance, however, should *never* be used as an excuse for activists to demand more company management focus on short-term results. Thus, to the extent that activists push for practices that simply would boost short-term stock price performance, I believe that *such* activism is wrong. Long-term thinking and sound corporate governance practices should *never* be mutually exclusive.

Corporate managements *should* indeed act in the best long-term interest of the company (and, by definition, its shareholders), even at the expense of short-term results. To the extent that any group of shareholders calls for management to do anything that goes against the long-term interest of the company for short-term benefit, such advice must be ignored.

That said, sometimes a shareholder activist's objective is to improve a target company's corporate culture. Admittedly, this is likely true only in a small minority of cases, but in those, I would applaud the presence of such an activist among a company's influential shareholders. An activist truly focused on improving the corporate culture must, by definition, be long-term oriented, and that is a positive influence.

Managements should do whatever they can to ignore the short-term noise, and focus on long-term success instead. That said, the best managements invest in long-term growth opportunities, but also return what they consider to be excess cash to shareholders. On this topic, the media and many observers tend to polarize the issue as to a simple choice between dividends and share repurchases. I like both, and there should be no reason to treat them as mutually exclusive; I favor what I call a balanced approach to shareholder remuneration.

A long-term orientation, again, is the key for me. This enables the investor to take full advantage of time horizon arbitrage (THA). One of the most important benefits that 'users' of THA have is that the real-time pricing and relative liquidity of the equity market enable them to choose the price at which they buy for the long run. Price volatility results in periodic dips, which create compelling long-term buying opportunities in great companies.

Long-term investors then don't have to sell at just *any* price. They can hold on to their stakes in excellent corporations and let the power of long-term compounding work for them (and potentially their heirs) through the incredible wealth-making machine that is the equity market.

Short-term trading, on the other hand, generates an obsession with quarterly results (and with 'macro' factors, such as the next move by the Fed). I agree with the new president of the Minneapolis Fed Neel Kashkari that too much time, effort (in a few words, intellectual capital) are wasted in trying to determine the very next move by the open markets committee of the Federal Reserve Board (the central bank of the US).

Perhaps a step in the right direction would be if all companies stopped issuing quarterly earnings guidance, a practice already embraced by a growing number of publicly traded corporations. Some of my allies in the quest against short-termism go as far as advocating the elimination of quarterly reporting requirements altogether. Based on that belief, companies would report data only for longer periods of time (such as semi-annual or so-called *interim* earnings results). I do not have a strong view on the subject, but if that is what it takes to ingrain more of a long-term orientation, I would be all for it.

*ETFs and when many stocks trade as one*

Even I have extolled the virtue of exchange-traded funds (ETFs), one of the few areas of customer-centric innovation by the financial industry in recent decades. Indeed, low-cost globally diversified ETFs are arguably the best way for investors without the time and passion for individual stock picking to invest for the long term.

Furthermore, let's make it clear that I do not believe in leveraged ETFs, and would not advocate inverse ETFs or narrowly focused instruments, for that matter. Also, as they represent baskets of stocks traded as a single security, in times of market turmoil, ETFs contribute to a phenomenon whereby very different stocks trade as if they were one and the same.

The ability of individual stocks to, in the long run, equate the net present value of a specific company's future cash flows gets obscured in the short term by all sorts of factors; hence the importance of *long-term* investing. The proliferation of ETFs, as investors have increasingly embraced them at the expense of individual company stocks, has exacerbated this phenomenon.

Unfortunately, in my opinion, to the extent that individual investors (particularly the younger ones) are involved in the US equity market, it is predominantly through ETFs. It is a pity that young investors are increasingly disinterested in individual shares. I believe stocks should be viewed as the pieces of companies they are; rather, all too often they are treated nowadays as just pieces of ETFs, which trade in the markets.

However, it has long been the case that even quite knowledgeable professional equity investors try to link too much the behavior of individual stocks to the performance of the US economy. Again, the longer your investment horizon, the less you should care about the short-term economic outlook for any one country.

Still, during macro-driven market-wide selloffs, correlations among individual stocks approach 1, meaning stocks all move in tandem, which results in the proverbial babies being thrown out with the bath water. This obviously creates buying opportunities for savvy long-term investors in individual stocks.

In the long run, in its 'weighing machine' role, the market will appraise individual company stocks as the net present value of the cash flows belonging to shareholders. The only difference is to whom those profits accrue. Fewer people (as a share of the American population) are investors in individual stocks than in earlier generations. Still, ETFs show a generally rising trend and, more importantly, the absolute number of investors globally continues to grow.

I am increasingly convinced that the generous profits from long-term investment in the US equity market will just find their way to the smartest, best-informed investors through the fungibility of money facilitated by THA.

The lesson of all the foregoing is for investors and companies alike to be long-term oriented. This is a key feature of the Alphabet corporate culture. It would behoove the financial industry to follow suit. Let's now turn our attention to another great corporate culture, but as we will see, not all that different from Alphabet's.

## CHAPTER SIX

### <u>Onward with Starbucks</u>

In one of the most labor-intensive industries, Starbucks (SBUX) manages to create incredible value over the long term by treating its partners, as it calls its tens of thousands of employees, better than companies in the more 'enlightened' knowledge economy. Starbucks hires many unskilled youths, yet treats them with utmost respect and dignity, gives them access to extraordinary benefits, which include stock ownership and tuition reimbursement, to help them broaden their long-term career opportunities, even well beyond their Starbucks years.

Howard Schultz, besides being an inspirational leader for one of the most wonderful corporate cultures ever as Starbucks CEO, is a prolific writer. His writings provide the reader a transparent view of the Starbucks corporate culture. His earlier book *Pour Your Heart into It: How Starbucks Built a Company One Cup at a Time* makes abundantly clear that, like in the case of Alphabet, long-term thinking is a cornerstone of the Starbucks corporate culture.

Schultz followed up that book with his candid thoughts on what happened with the company the following decade in *Onward.* Both are extremely useful reading for anybody interested in the topic of corporate culture, but the earlier book is almost a how-to guide to becoming an excellent manager, in my view.

As I will show through quotes of Schultz himself, long-term thinking is a key component of the Starbucks culture. So is caring for the companies' partners. In *Pour Your Heart into It,* Schultz says "If there's one accomplishment I'm proudest of at Starbucks, it's the relationship of trust and confidence we've built with the people who work at the company. That's not just an empty phrase, as it is at so many companies."

The extraordinary employee benefits Starbucks offers, even to part-timers, is certainly proof of that. Schultz goes on to say. "These policies and attitudes run counter to conventional business wisdom. A company that is managed only for the benefit of shareholders treats its employees as a line item, a cost to be contained."

The Starbucks chairman and CEO goes on to make the following key point. "What many in business don't realize is that it's not a zero-sum game. Treating employees benevolently shouldn't be viewed as an added cost that cuts into profits, but as a powerful energizer that can grow the enterprise into something far greater than one leader could envision. With pride in their work, Starbucks people are less likely to leave. Our turnover rate is less than half the industry average, which not only saves money but strengthens our bond with customers."

The earlier a leader tries to imprint a particular culture in a company's history, the better. Of course, this is a luxury few corporate managers can enjoy, and it was indeed an advantage that both Schultz and the Alphabet cofounders had over many other companies. In the words of Schultz "...as a parent, or as an entrepreneur, you begin imprinting your beliefs from Day One, whether you realize it or not. Once the children, or the people of the company, have absorbed those values, you can't suddenly change their world view with a lecture on ethics.

It's difficult, if not impossible, to reinvent a company's culture. If you have made the mistake of doing business one way for five years, you can't suddenly impose a layer of different values upon it. By then, the water's already in the well, and you have to drink it.

Whatever your culture, your values, your guiding principles, you have to take steps to inculcate them in the organization early in its life so that they can guide every decision, every hire, every strategic objective you set. Whether you are the CEO or a lower level employee, the single most important thing you do at work each day is communicate your values to others, especially new hires. Establishing the right tone at the inception of an enterprise, whatever its size, is vital to its long-term success."

I most definitely agree with Schultz; culture is key to long-term corporate performance, and this is key to long-term *stock* performance. The Starbucks chief goes on to say. "As you build, you never know which decisions will end up being the cornerstones. Each one adds so much value later on, and you're not cognizant of it at the time.

Don't underestimate the importance of the early signals you send out in the course of building your enterprise and imprinting your values upon it. When you take on a partner, and when you select employees, be sure to choose people who share your mission with like-minded souls, it will have a far greater impact...

But my view of a successful business wasn't just measured in number of stores. I wanted to create a brand name respected for the best in coffee and a well-run company admired for its corporate responsibility. I wanted to elevate the enterprise to a higher standard, to make sure our people proud of working for a company that cared for them and gave back to their community...

I wanted to build a company that would thrive for years because its competitive advantage was based on its values and guiding principles. I wanted to attract and hire individuals who worked together with a single purpose, who avoided political infighting and loved reaching for goals others thought impossible. I wanted to create a culture in which the endgame was not only personal gratification but a respected and admired enterprise."

This, in my opinion, is exactly what Howard Schultz has accomplished at Starbucks. The visionary leader goes on to say. "The bigger Starbucks grows, the more chance that some employee, somewhere, isn't getting the respect he or she deserves. If we can't attend to that problem, we are facing a failure worse than any shortcomings Wall Street can detect." Again, I could not agree more!

Schultz adds. "I know, in my heart, if we treat people as a line item under expenses, we're not living up to our goals and our values.

Their passion and devotion is our number-one competitive advantage. Lose it, and we've lost the game." The long-term focus that is a cornerstone of the Starbucks culture is evident from their mantra of "investing ahead of the growth curve." In addition, Schultz writes about his initial concern about approaching venture capital investors way before the company went public. "At first, I was wary of taking this step, for I had heard that some venture capitalists intrude on entrepreneurial ventures and ultimately ruin them with short-term thinking."

Besides an almost obsessive focus on the long term, the Starbucks and Alphabet cultures share a mantra of inspiring people to hire others better than themselves. Schultz devotes an entire chapter of *Pour Your Heart into It* to the subject. In his own words, "strong, creative people are a lot more stimulating to be around than yes-men. What can you learn from those who know less than you? They may massage your ego for a while and take orders easily, but they won't help you grow." Remember the concept of "smart creatives" at Alphabet?

Schultz then goes on to talk about some key hires in the late 1980s. "I tried to make the message I sent to them – and by extension, to the entire company – as unequivocal as possible: 'I hired you because you're smarter than I am. Now go and prove it.'"

Hiring only people smarter than yourself is an intimidating challenge for most people, let alone to leaders of companies they control. Making it part of the culture is thus most commendable, but the Starbucks and Alphabet case studies suggest it is a key ingredient of a winning corporate culture. Legendary investor Warren Buffett also favors it as a preferred practice.

Where Alphabet and Starbucks seem to most 'clash' with traditional Wall Street practices is in the companies' insistence that they cannot yield when investors seem to most demand short-term results.

Schultz writes a chapter in *Pour Your Heart into It* titled "Wall Street Measures a Company's Price, Not Its Value." Therein, in relating the process of choosing investment banks to lead the company's IPO, he talks about his experience with Wall Street analysts as follows. "Almost all of them seemed to tune out when I started discussing our company's Mission Statement. If they were taking notes, their pens stopped moving when I brought up values, as if I were indulging in rhetoric unrelated to Starbucks' financial performance. Experience has taught me that it's easy to talk about values, hard to implement them, and even harder for an outsider to determine which values are heartfelt and which are window-dressing. Wall Street cannot place a value on values."

This passage is at the heart of the need for this book. Wall Street **needs** a way to start placing a value on values. Schultz then writes. "These people were from a different world, where everything was weighted by its financial value; if you couldn't put a number on it, it didn't show up in the equation. They wanted to know what we could deliver to shareholders, not how we treated our employees." The failure by Wall Street to see this important link is to blame for much of the prevailing short-term thinking among corporate managements. Schultz, in trying to convince investors to think otherwise, says the following.

"But, I told them, Starbucks was attempting to accomplish something more ambitious than just grow a profitable enterprise. We had a mission, to educate consumers everywhere about fine coffee. We had a vision, to create an atmosphere in our stores that drew people in and gave them a sense of wonder and romance in the midst of their harried lives. We had an idealistic dream, that our company could be far more than the paradigm identified by corporate America in the past. I told them about Bean Stock, our revolutionary new program of granting stock options to all employees. Our first priority was to take care of our people, because they were the ones responsible for communicating our passion to our customers. If we did that well, we'd accomplish our second priority, taking care of our customers. And only if we achieved both of those goals would we be able to provide long-term value for our shareholders." That is exactly what Starbucks (and Alphabet) have indeed done!

Of course it is to some extent easier to focus on the long run when you leading a company that is in a new or emerging industry (versus a mature one), and where the sky seems the limit to the long-term potential. This has certainly been the case for both Alphabet and Starbucks, and the long-term orientation of their corporate cultures has undoubtedly been key to their extraordinary success.

Howard Schultz muses about the difficult challenges his young company faced in the late 1980s when it was still losing money. He, however, had a strong conviction that his then small company had to prepare itself for a time not far away when it would be far larger. By thinking big, a self-fulfilling prophecy of sorts was at play, and this is yet another important parallel to the Alphabet corporate culture (as what Larry Page terms 'moonshot' thinking).

It is staggering how two companies which operate in such different businesses share such similar cultures. In the words of Starbucks' Howard Schultz in *Pour Your Heart into It,* "... the story of Starbucks is not just a record of growth and success. It's also about how a company can be built in a different way...It's living proof that a company can lead with its heart and nurture its soul and still make money. It shows a company can provide long-term value for shareholders without sacrificing its core belief in treating its employees with respect and dignity, both because we have a team of leaders who believe it's right and because it's the best way to do business."

Perhaps, Schultz is being too modest. Starbucks (not unlike Alphabet) has created extraordinary wealth for its shareholders while doing right by its employees (partners in Schultz lingo). These are socially conscious companies that care for *all* stakeholders, and in the end, their own *shareholders* have done better than those at most other companies. Their unique (but similar to each other) corporate culture has undoubtedly contributed to a long-standing (and thus, likely sustainable) valuation premium. I strongly believe that, in the long run (where it really matters), the interests of all stakeholders (shareholders, workers and customers) converge.

The fact that similar companies in similar industries with similar financial results and growth rates can trade at very different valuation multiples is, to me at least, further proof that there is something conventional analysis misses -- the quality of the corporate culture. Starbucks is a key example of a stock that seems to always trade at a valuation premium, which I would have to define as a *corporate culture premium.*

Such a valuation premium, particularly when one does not understand corporate culture at all, can be a big attraction to short sellers. Even as early as *Pour Your Heart into It,* Schultz wrote about it as follows. "Over the past few years, we've faced many a skeptic in the financial community. Starbucks' stock has always traded at a high multiple to earnings, which has made it a favorite for short-sellers, who bet against it because they are convinced that our company is over-valued. Since 1992, we've had the dubious honor of consistently being one of the top names on the short-sellers' list. But, so far, most of our steadfast believers have been rewarded, and the skeptics have been proven wrong."

Analysts and investors only looking at traditional, conventional valuation metrics just cannot wrap their heads around the valuation premium that the markets rightfully award to companies with superior corporate cultures. Therefore, I have come to the conclusion that there is a need to assess a company's culture in order to try to value values (in the words of Howard Schultz); a corporate culture scorecard should help investors to assign a corporate culture premium, where warranted. Given that Alphabet has advanced to the top of the global market value rankings in record time, I propose that its own prescriptions for corporate culture provide the most actionable toolkit to evaluate the key feature of company DNA.

The fact that Google's history is so brief means that the lessons it provides are all quite recent. Therefore, the questions I recommend in the next chapter for broadly assessing the quality of a corporate culture are based on the advice that Laszlo Bock, Alphabet's head of people operations, generously shares in his recent book *WORK RULES!* This very useful text's byline, "insights from inside Google that will transform how you live and learn," as well as passages throughout the book, make it patently clear that Bock wants as many entities as possible to embrace and attempt to mimic the lessons from the rapid evolution of this great company.

I certainly am (and would argue, market participants in general should be) extremely grateful to Alphabet and to Bock himself for their 'open platform' mantra. Their willingness to share with the rest of the world what has served Alphabet so well is invaluable. Essentially, the Google DNA provides a yardstick (even more, a wish list) for the quality of a company's corporate culture. In terms of equity analysis, my goal is to use Alphabet's prescriptions, as explained by Bock, to contribute to expanding the existing arsenal of the global investor. The corporate culture questionnaire I am hereby introducing should be used, in conjunction with more traditional valuation metrics, to evaluate the long-term prospects of a company and its stock.

# CHAPTER SEVEN

## 'Google' a New Corporate Quality Questionnaire: The Corporate Culture Assessment Tool (CAT)

Alphabet (still widely known by the name of its key division, Google) is just this year reaching adulthood in human years, barely 18 years old! This very young company, however, has become this year the most valuable corporate entity in the universe by stock market value. In my opinion, what allowed this relatively new company to achieve this feat was indeed its unique corporate culture.

Laszlo Bock, in *WORK RULES!* follows in the great tradition set by Google executive chairman Eric Schmidt and the company's former SVP of Products Jonathan Rosenberg with their own *How Google Works* of sharing invaluable insights from Alphabet with the rest of the world. My intention is to attempt to condense all their key lessons to constitute the core of a broad framework to evaluate corporate culture at different companies.

At the outset, I must reiterate the following caveat. The fact that the key Google lessons for exceptional corporate culture have all been learned so recently is both an advantage and a disadvantage. On the plus side, the lessons are obviously fresh and current. On the minus side, though, Alphabet has enjoyed a unique situation in that its extraordinary culture was imprinted right from the start of the company, which itself was much more recent than that of most corporations.

Thus, many will question the applicability of what has been learned at and from Google to the broad universe of companies.

Like Laszlo Bock, I do believe that most of what characterizes the key attributes of the Alphabet corporate culture can indeed be applied to most other companies by a committed leadership team. Undoubtedly, the challenge is a lot tougher for 'old' firms with an entrenched 'dysfunctional' culture. Yet, it is far from impossible to dramatically improve a corporate culture, and in my view, very well worth the effort in terms of long-term value creation.

I must admit that Starbucks' Howard Schultz, who like the Google cofounders was able to imprint wonderful values at his company from early on, does think it is extremely difficult to *change* a corporate culture. My own practice of using DNA as a synonym for corporate culture also makes this point clear. Still, a good starting point is to grade or assess an existing corporate culture. From there, a leadership team truly committed to change and improvement can indeed start moving a company in a better direction. So let's get into the cultural evaluation framework inspired by Google.

In his book *WORK RULES!*, Laszlo Bock notes that in its early years, Google came up with "'10 Things We Know to Be True,' a list of ten beliefs that guide how we run our business." Here they are: "Focus on the user and all else will follow. It's best to do one thing really, really well. Fast is better than slow. Democracy on the Web works. You don't need to be at your desk to need an answer. You can make money without doing evil. There's always more information out there. The need for information crosses all borders. You can be serious without a suit. Great just isn't good enough." The corporate culture scorecard I propose would have, as its backbone, a list of questions to ask from a company's management and employees at all levels of the organization. The key questions are broadly aligned with the chapters of Laszlo Bock's book.

The first couple of questions have to do with the opening chapter of *WORK RULES!* on employees acting as founders. **How far 'down' the organization does the company give employees access to equity?** A key feature of both Alphabet and Starbucks is that the rank and file get company stock.

The alignment of interests accomplished by *all-employee* ownership of equity in the company does wonders in terms of corporate culture. According to Bock in the first chapter of his seminal book, "Building an exceptional team or institution starts with a founder. But being a founder doesn't mean starting a new company. It is within anyone's grasp to be the founder and culture-creator of their own team, whether you are the first employee or joining a company that has existed for decades."

Bock goes on to say. "One of my hopes in writing this book is that anyone reading it starts thinking of themselves as a founder. Maybe not of an entire company, but the founder of a team, a family, a culture. The fundamental lesson from Google's experience is that you must first choose whether you want to be a founder or an employee. It's not a question of literal ownership. It's a question of attitude."

Therefore, the next question in the culture scorecard is **Do the company's employees feel they are more than that, simple employees?** Starbucks calls them partners, Alphabet's are Googlers. While these are just names, do the company's employees *truly* feel like they are treated better than just line items to control in a profit and loss (P&L) statement? Are they more than just a number? As Bock concludes, "And the greatest founders create room for other founders to build alongside them."

The second chapter in *WORK RULES!* is titled "Culture Eats Strategy for Breakfast." If you have read this far, you know I agree with that statement! I believe the chapter's byline is just as correct. "If you give people freedom, they will amaze you."

Alphabet even has a chief culture officer! Bock writes "you have to explore the three defining aspects of our culture: mission, transparency, and voice. Google's mission is the first cornerstone of our culture." While most large corporations claim to have one embodied in their mission statement, my experience is that, in most cases, such a statement is little more than words.

Many companies do not tend to adhere to their mission statement, and most of their employees would not be able to articulate it. Therefore, the next set of questions is **Can you, in your own** *words, tell us what your company's mission statement is; does the company really live by its mission; does this company mission give your own work meaning?*

Bock goes on to say. "Transparency is the second cornerstone of our culture. 'Default to open' is a phrase sometimes heard in the open-source technology community...We share everything, and trust Googlers to keep information confidential."

While Alphabet is a very open company in many ways, there are obviously many things that Googlers should not share with the outside world, lest the company risk some of its competitive advantages. The company trusts employees to keep what should stay inside Alphabet there, and shares with Googlers as much information as possible. A key question for our corporate culture scorecard is thus *Do you feel your company trusts you with key information about how and what it is doing?*

Referring to the third defining aspect of Alphabet's culture, Bock writes "Voice is the third cornerstone of Google's culture. Voice means giving employees a real say in how the company is run. Either you believe people are good and you welcome their input, or you don't. For many organizations this is terrifying, but it is the only way to live in adherence to your values."

Questions to try to assess this cultural trait would be *Do you feel the company values your input; does the company listen to its employees?* Bock concludes this key chapter on culture with the following statement. "Give people slightly more trust, freedom and authority than you are comfortable giving them. If you're not nervous, you haven't given them enough."

Starbucks' Schultz already taught us to hire people who are smarter than we are. Alphabet also lives by this cultural trait. In the words of Bock, "Only hire people who are better than you." This is obviously challenging to implement and more time consuming; Bock expands. "In addition to being willing to take longer, to wait for someone better than you, you also need managers to give up power when it comes to hiring."

Alphabet asks as many Googlers as possible to get involved in the critical process of hiring, and uses committees rather than the single supervising manager to make the hiring decision. Bock also expands on the definition of looking for the best. "It's about finding the very best people who will be successful in the context of your organization, and who will make everyone around them more successful."

One of the key reasons for Alphabet's astonishing success is that it empowers Googlers."20% time" is a key part of this cultural attribute. In the chapter entitled "Let the Inmates Run the Asylum," Bock says. "'Does your manager trust you?' is a profound question. If you believe people are fundamentally good, and if your organization is able to hire well, there is nothing to fear from giving your people freedom.

Remember that the primary definition of 'asylum' is a 'place of refuge.' One of the nobler aspirations of a workplace should be that it's a place of refuge where people are free to create, build, and grow. Why not let the inmates run the asylum?

The first step to mass empowerment is making it safe for people to speak up. In Japan there's a saying: *Deru kugi wa utareru*. 'The stake that sticks up gets hammered down.' It's a warning to conform.

This is why we take as much power away from managers as we can. The less formal authority they have, the fewer carrots and sticks they have to lord over their teams, and the more latitude the teams have to innovate." A key question therefore is **Do you feel trusted and empowered by your company?**

Another important statement Bock makes, with which I fully agree is. "Workplaces that permit employees more freedom tap into the natural intrinsic motivation, which in turn helps employees feel even more autonomous and capable." In *WORK RULES!* the author also advises to expect much from your employees.

Therefore, the next natural question is **Do you feel your company trusts you to do great work and give you the freedom to accomplish it?** A logical follow-up would be **Is your company's performance appraisal methodology fair and do you feel there are advancement opportunities for good performers in this company?**

In empowering their people, companies should also implicitly give them 'permission to fail'. In Bock's words, "The biggest lesson was that rewarding smart failure was vital to support a culture of risk-taking." He adds, concluding with a statement from cofounder Page "And if people shoot for the stars and only hit the moon, don't treat them too harshly. Ease the pain of failure to leave room for learning. As Larry often says: If your goals are ambitious and crazy enough, even failure will be a pretty good achievement."

The next chapter in Bock's book explains how many of Alphabet's key employee benefits are a lot less costly to the company than people think. The byline to the title reads "Most of Google's people programs can be duplicated by anyone." Thus, companies don't need to start out being as successful as Alphabet to be able to treat their employees great.

Bock says: "We use our people programs to achieve three goals: efficiency, community, and innovation. Every one of our programs exists to further at least one of these goals, and often more than one." A lot of these Alphabet employee benefits come from employee suggestions. Therefore, the next key point Bock makes is "It's very easy to find reasons to say no. But it's the wrong answer because it shuts down both employee voice and the chance to learn something new.

Find ways to say yes.

Employees will reward you by making your workplace more vibrant, fun, and productive."

He adds later. "This is the secret to our culture. So much of it is grassroots-driven. The performers are in charge of the circus." Many of benefits Alphabet offers its Googlers are employee-driven. Its generous death benefits to employees' survivors were highlighted in Bock's book as he cites a *Forbes* article for which he was interviewed ("Here's What Happens to Google Employees When They Die."). Says Bock "The response was enormous and the article was quickly viewed almost half a million times.

Once word was out, I immediately heard from my peers at other companies. The number one question was, 'Doesn't that cost a fortune?

Not even close. Our cost thus far has been running at about one-tenth of one percent of payroll. Put another way, the average US company spends 4 percent a year on salary increases: roughly 3 percent for annual increases and 1 percent for promotions. I bet if you asked any employee if they'd want a program like this at the price of getting a 2.9 percent raise instead of a 3.0 percent raise, almost all would say yes." In our scorecard we could ask ***How pleased are you with your employee benefits; how open is your company to benefit suggestions by you or your fellow employees?***

Further talking about culture, Bock writes. "Whether you're part of a large organization or a small one, you may as well be thoughtful about the environment you create. Our goal is to nudge in a direction that Googlers would agree makes their lives better, not by taking away choice but by making it easier to make good choices."

As far as dealing with adversity, Bock notes. "Admit your mistake. Be transparent about it; Take counsel from all directions; Fix whatever broke; Find the moral in the mistake, and teach it."

In his concluding chapter, Bock explains. "Throughout this book I've offered short lists of 'work rules' in each chapter, in case you want to focus on one area or another. But if you want to become a high-freedom environment, here are the ten steps that will transform your team or workplace:

1. Give your work meaning.
2. Trust your people.
3. Hire only people who are better than you.
4. Don't confuse development with managing performance.
5. Focus on the two tails.
6. Be frugal and generous.
7. Pay unfairly.
8. Nudge.
9. Manage rising expectations.
10. Enjoy! And then go back to No. 1 and start again."

Please read all of *WORK RULES!* to better understand the key features behind the Alphabet culture of success. For now, Bock also quotes Netflix's Reed Hastings. As I mentioned earlier, the video streaming and content company is another example of a great corporate culture. As Bock notes in quoting Hastings, "Responsible people thrive on freedom and are worthy of freedom. Our model is to increase employee freedom as we grow, rather than limit it, to continue to attract and nourish innovative people, so we have a better chance of sustained success."

We have heretofore focused primarily on two companies with exceptionally great corporate cultures, Alphabet and Starbucks. Both of these, though now quite large (and in the case of the former, the very largest company in the world by market cap), are relatively young entities. Google is turning just eighteen, and Starbucks 45, even if we use 1971 as the founding date. The visionary leaders of these companies have been there from the beginning, thus at the earliest opportunity imprinting on them their unique values.

The case of Starbucks is just a bit different, as Howard Schultz acquired his former employer in 1987, when the company he had recently founded (*Il Giornale*) and Starbucks itself were both still very small entrepreneurial companies. For all practical purposes, we can say Schultz has involved at what we now know as Starbucks from its beginning.

Taking that as a given, both Starbucks and Alphabet are still run by the leaders who imprinted onto them their culture from early on. Most companies have a corporate culture that has evolved over many more years, leaders, and in many cases, leadership styles. I have already hinted at the fact that the more ingrained a dysfunctional culture is, the more challenging it is to transform it into a winning corporate culture.

But I have also stated that, like Alphabet's Laszlo Bock, I do not believe it is *impossible* to meaningfully improve a corporate culture, particularly if the leadership team is truly committed to change. *Change* is the operative word. This can obviously come about in several ways. Often, a management change is necessary. The old leadership team must go, and a new, visionary CEO comes in to implement a new vision.

Change sometimes comes about through a corporate takeover. A large, well known legendary American blue-chip company, Anheuser Busch, has seen its corporate culture transformed in recent years following its takeover by InBev. The culture of the world's largest brewer, Anheuser-Busch InBev, is actually the DNA of the acquiring entity.

The winning culture that a small team of executives imprinted on Companhia Cervejaria Brahma (Brahma), a Brazilian beer company after they acquired it, was the genesis of what is now the culture of AB InBev (BUD). A flat, meritocratic organization without a myriad of status symbols (a characteristic, by the way, that Alphabet shares) and an almost obsessive focus on economic value creation are landmarks of this winning culture.

# CHAPTER EIGHT

## *Corporate Culture Changes in Mid-Course*

### The Power of Big Dreams – The AB InBev (R)evolution

We have learned that the cultures of Alphabet and Starbucks encourage their people to shoot for the stars. Another company that has turned big dreams into reality is what is now BUD. The company as we know it started out when the three founding partners of what is now 3G Capital, leading a turnaround team, acquired Brahma in Brazil.

Subsequently, they acquired their largest Brazilian rival (Antarctica) to form AmBev. They followed this with the purchase of Argentina's Quilmes, then combining with Belgium's Interbrew to create InBev, which ultimately acquired Anheuser Busch to create today's AB InBev. Talk about global aspirations turned into reality!

But big dreams must team up with a powerful corporate culture to actually materialize. As I stated at the outset, I favor a purposeful, results-oriented, mission-driven culture that provides a supportive environment in which employees want to do great work aligned with the broader company mission. To achieve this, employees must understand the company's mission and truly believe in it.

Like Alphabet's, AB InBev's mission is incredibly simple. In their own words, "At AB InBev, our dream is to be the Best Beer Company Bringing People Together For a Better World." This is very easy for employees to understand and buy into. Again, while many companies tout their mission, far fewer truly live by it. AB InBev does. Going back to the Brahma days, I had the opportunity to talk to many of the company's employees, and there was always a common message.

This is what AB InBev now (truly) claims. "What really brings our strategy together is our Dream-People-Culture platform which is rooted in our 10 Principles and is the driving force behind our culture and everything we stand for as a company. Despite having operations in many countries around the world, with different national cultures, we operate as one company, with one Dream and one culture to unite us, and a clear focus on having the right people in the right place at the right time.

Our culture is built on ownership, informality, candor, transparency and meritocracy. We set ourselves stretch targets and are never completely satisfied with our results.

Our culture not only defines who we are, but also provides the energy and the focus to drive forward and achieve our Dream to be the Best Beer Company Bringing People Together For a Better World."

From the company's website, here is how they lay out their ten principles.

 Our shared dream energizes everyone to work in the same direction to be the:
**Best Beer Company**
**Bringing People Together**
**For a Better World**

 Our greatest strength is our people. Great People grow at the pace of their talent and are rewarded accordingly.

We recruit, develop and retain people who can be better than ourselves. We will be judged by the quality of our teams.

We are never completely satisfied with our results, which are the fuel of our company. Focus and zero-complacency guarantee lasting competitive advantage.

The consumer is the Boss. We serve our consumers by offering brand experiences that play a meaningful role in their lives, and always in a responsible way.

We believe common sense and simplicity are usually better guidelines than unnecessary sophistication and complexity.

We are a company of owners. Owners take results personally.

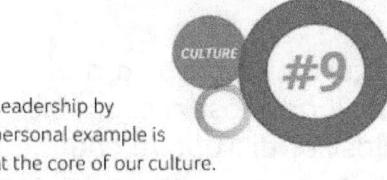 We manage our costs tightly, to free up resources that will support sustainable and profitable top line growth.

Leadership by personal example is at the core of our culture. We do what we say.

We never take shortcuts. Integrity, hard work, quality, and responsibility are key to building our company.

Even the way AB InBev lays out its guiding principles highlights the importance to management of their unique corporate culture. In my opinion, it is this unique DNA that has enabled AB InBev to become not only the best, but by far the largest, beer company in the world. In the case of this exemplary company, dramatic change at what was the US's largest beer company (Anheuser Busch) had to come about through its acquisition by InBev.

**Cultures in Flux**

Existing internal management can also effect transformational change. It is a cultural feature of my next corporate example that has allowed it to reinvent itself to deal with immense technological and market disruption. As I indicated earlier, Netflix's corporate culture makes it incredibly resilient. I came across the presentation in the link below by Netflix's CEO Reed Hastings through *WORK RULES!* It highlights the importance to Hastings of his company's culture.

For more information on the Netflix corporate culture, please refer to http://www.slideshare.net/reed2001/culture-1798664

The Netflix winning culture has enabled the company to succeed beyond most reasonable expectations in the midst of disruptive change. What it highlights is that certain cultural traits can allow a company to deal better with an adverse environment than most others. In more stable environments, a different type of culture may serve a company better. Change in any case is part and parcel of all cultures, in that they are never fully static. The key is for the core of a positive culture to remain even as the rest of it gradually molds itself to fit the changing times.

A company whose DNA seems to embrace change is another of my favorites in terms of corporate culture, Nike (NKE). According to CEO Mark Parker in a November 7, 2012 Business Insider article citing an interview by Fast Company, "Our management approach hasn't come from studying and reading business books. It's more intuitive, from the culture of sports. We're constantly looking for ways to improve. How do you adapt to your environment and really focus on your potential? To really go after that, you have to embrace the reality that it is not going to slow down. And you have to look at that as half full, not half empty."

"Companies and people look at the pace of change as a challenge, an obstacle, a hurdle, .... we like to look at it as opportunity: Get on the offense."

There is much more yet to learn from the Nike corporate culture. I must admit that what most attracted me to it in the first place was that Starbucks' Howard Schultz is himself a big fan of Nike cofounder Phil Knight. Unfortunately, Mr. Knight's book *Shoe Dog* came out too late for inclusion here. In general, though, my own book itself represents a work in progress. Like with Alphabet's 'launch and iterate' philosophy, I want to put the thoughts out there for 'crowdsourcing' to build on the concepts. I have great hopes for the participants and graduates of Young Investors Society to contribute to the research and development of the study of corporate cultures.

For now, the Business Insider article on Nike's culture goes on to say: "Parker's strategy is to embrace and adapt to the environment, to aggressively change with it rather than simply weathering it." Thus, winning cultures more often than not appear to at the very least not fear change.

An industry that arguably seems to want things *not* to change is that of my former employers, financial services providers. I would argue that there is a confidence crisis surrounding the financial industry, which seems more derided than ever by the general public.

*Sometimes internal change at the top is needed to effect a cultural change*

As I already explained, Alphabet and Starbucks have indeed benefitted from the fact that their respective extraordinary cultures have evolved over a short period of time, and where their long-time visionary leaders responsible for those cultures are still very much involved nowadays. Companies with ingrained, rather dysfunctional cultures that were put in place many decades ago face a much more difficult challenge to dramatically improve their cultures.

Anheuser-Busch eventually became an acquisition target, and the current culture of AB InBev is a reflection of that of the acquiring InBev. In some other cases, an internal change at the helm of the company presents an opportunity to effect meaningful cultural change. In such cases, a management change is a necessary but not sufficient catalyst for true cultural evolution.

Many of the largest and best-known American corporations have gone through a number of leadership transitions over decades. Leaders with strong personalities have an ability to mold corporate cultures to fit their style, and the DNA of a well-known company today may well be completely different than what it displayed in its early decades or even just a couple of decades ago.

I believe this is the case of the Walt Disney Company. In 2005, Bob Iger replaced Michael Eisner as CEO of the media and entertainment conglomerate. Eisner was known as an overly controlling executive. According to Wikipedia, Roy E. Disney (son of cofounder Roy O. Disney) resigned from his positions as the company's vice chairman and chairman of Walt Disney Feature Animation in 2003 "accusing Eisner of micromanagement, flops with the ABC television network, timidity in the theme park business, turning the Walt Disney Company into a 'rapacious, soul-less' company, and refusing to establish a clear succession plan, as well as a string of box-office movie flops starting in the year 2000."

A more recent example is Walmart (WMT). I believe the corporate culture of the retailing giant had become dysfunctional. Doug McMillon replaced Mike Duke, becoming the company's president and CEO in February, 2014. While I would by no means like to imply that Duke made WMT's culture dysfunctional, the succession of CEOs that followed founder Sam Walton in that position did affect the culture at what had been a company with torrid growth. The fact is that McMillon inherited a situation in which WMT's culture and reputation had been tarnished on several fronts.

Contrary to what is the case at Starbucks and Costco (and what has historically been widely believed to be true at Whole Foods), Walmart became known as a company that treated its employees (associates) less than fairly. McMillon has admitted as much by implementing a ground-breaking program of 'investing in people' of late. In October 2015 the stock of the retailing giant experienced substantial weakness, as what I then wrote illustrates.

Walmart (WMT) experienced one of its worst trading sessions in decades as the largest brick and mortar retailer detailed its expectations at an analyst meeting in the NYSE for the results of the next couple of years. Months ago, WMT had already announced meaningful changes to its employee compensation policies. Under new leadership, the retailing giant has been revamping stores, to address prior underinvestment, and finally started the long process of reversing the generalized perception that it has not been treating employees particularly well.

The broad-based increase in wages going all the way down to starting pay for unskilled workers was bound to significantly increase the company's labor bill. Thus, following a first full year decline in earnings, WMT expects stable earnings for the following year, and growth only in the next. According to the company, fully three fourths of the increase in expected costs are related to labor.

Longer term, if WMT's new management executes well on its strategy, both revenues and profits should improve versus where they would have been if the retailer had continued to operate in the old way. The experience of companies such as Costco (COST) and Starbucks (SBUX) highlights that treating and compensating employees fairly does result in better revenue and profit performance in the long run. In addition to guidance for $80 billion in free cash flow over the next three years, WMT also announced plans to repurchase $20 billion of its shares during the same period.

A couple of days after the initial decline in its stock, I followed up with this. Walmart continues to see its stock struggle in the aftermath of its analyst meeting earlier this week. There are two major themes emerging in much of the public commentary since the stock's initial double-digit percentage plunge. Other than the typical short-term focus that has become the norm in much of the analysis of publicly-traded equities, the major ramifications and extrapolations that people are making are that (a) there has been an inflection point away from traditional bricks and mortar retailing; and (b) the labor cost pressures at WMT will spread well beyond that retailer.

Amazon (AMZN), a company on which I have written favorably before, is indeed a great disruptor, and WMT will continue to evolve most aspects of the way it does business to continue to be a successful retailer well into the future. Yet, the pendulum of investor sentiment always swings too far, and rumors of WMT's demise are exaggerated. The changes the company has been making in the last few months (and explained in further detail at the analyst meeting) are for the better, and meaningfully increase the probabilities that the company will thrive in the long run. The worst for WMT is behind it, not ahead of it. The 'omni-channel' retailing strategy on which WMT is starting to execute -- while challenging and costly to implement well -- will likely be the way of the future, for many years to come.

The other 'concern' regarding WMT's new approach towards labor may be more valid, but only to a limited extent. There are growing signs that the share of labor in the profit pie is bottoming out. For companies 'underpaying' their employees, this implies a meaningfully larger labor bill going forward. For companies that have been at the forefront of treating their employees fairly, however, the change is likely to be negligible. This is one reason why I have traditionally focused on companies with a great, purposeful culture for the core of my portfolio.

The companies with strong cultures in the core of my portfolio treat their employees well. Motivated, well taken care of employees contribute to a great consumer experience that makes the company successful in the long run. It all converges into great long-term stock price performance. Starbucks (SBUX) is a key core holding of mine, and a great example of this. In the retailing space, Costco (COST) immediately comes to mind. Apple (AAPL), my largest holding by far, is another key example. The company recently extended stock grants all the way down its labor ladder.

Finally, restauranteur Danny Meyer recently announced ground-breaking changes at his Union Square Hospitality Group restaurants – a no-tipping policy implemented together with significant menu price increases that will include the service charge to be distributed all the way to the dish washing personnel. The higher menu prices at Meyer's restaurants will enable the company to offer incentive variable compensation to all employees.

These are but a few recent examples of what to me implies that the share of labor in the profit pie is bottoming out. This does not mean that stock prices will suffer as a result. I expect quite the contrary to be the case. The fact that even WMT entry-level employees will be making more money will provide additional fuel for consumption, the lifeblood of US GDP. Workers will be getting a bigger slice but of a yet larger pie. Strong consumers in the long run mean even stronger profits and higher stock prices. I do not believe that labor cost pressures will be such that there will be any meaningful labor-push inflation. They will simply represent an offsetting factor to deflationary forces, resulting in the benign reflationary environment I see for the intermediate term.

These developments highlight a broader trend currently at play that remains underappreciated, in my view. Following many years in which labor's share of the profit pie had been in secular decline, the nation's workers are starting to regain bargaining power, and I expect the labor share of the profit pool to rise in the coming years.

This is a trend already in place (through market forces) without the likely interventionism that some of the current political rhetoric advocates. Social trends in and of themselves, aided by the forces of supply and demand, are pushing for more benign labor conditions economy-wide. As this trend takes hold on its own, I expect a more socially conscious corporate ownership democracy to gradually entrench itself. Again, the key is to focus on the long term.

As I have explained, contrary to successful corporate DNAs, such as that of Alphabet and Starbucks, the culture of the financial industry tends to be much more short-term oriented, despite occasional lip service to the contrary. Winning cultures that emphasize sharing success with employees at every level of the organization and focusing on the long term tend to (perhaps coincidentally) also emphasize giving beyond the firm itself. Social consciousness, it happens, tends to be a cornerstone of all winning cultures I know.

Another common feature among positive corporate cultures is that their companies tend to be learning organizations. Starting with a management philosophy that encourages employees to hire people smarter than themselves, companies with successful cultures appear avid to be always learning more to become increasingly better (not necessarily bigger). Alphabet and Starbucks share this key cultural trait.

Yet, in terms of their broader approach to hiring employees, these two companies with exemplary cultures could arguably not be more different from each other. Alphabet is known to be more selective than 'Ivy League' universities when it comes to the percentage of applicants that they admit into their ranks.

Starbucks, on the other hand, believes in hiring people that many other companies would reject. Needless to say, the business of Starbucks is a lot more labor intensive than that of Alphabet. The nature of the companies' work is also completely different.

The key take-away here is that companies with very different employee needs and business focus can nonetheless have similarly successful and favorable corporate cultures.

### Embrace change...or else!

As much as the financial industry is criticized for its lobbying efforts in congress, as I have explained, I think they need to spend a lot more of their time, energy and resources explaining themselves to the population at large. Unfortunately, in my opinion, the general culture of the financial services industry seems to instead feature trying to present themselves as smarter than the general public.

By turning ever more esoteric, trying to sound increasingly 'scientific' and thus distancing itself ever more from the average person on the street, the financial industry does itself much more harm than good. How can a culture that essentially emphasizes setting the firm's employees apart from the general public as much as possible succeed in the long run?

It appears to me as the opposite of what is evident at companies with winning cultures, such as Starbucks. The closer a company is to its customers, the better it can relate to its users, the better for its long-term performance on all fronts. Starbucks does indeed put the customer at the top of its priority list, and as I said earlier, it and Alphabet seem obsessed with delighting their ultimate clients. This is clearly not what the financial industry is generally known for.

The Starbucks corporate culture, while always evolving, has remained true to its *core* throughout the tenure of Howard Schultz. As the different tones of his books *Pour Your Heart into It* and *Onward* highlight, nonetheless, there was a time in between those books when Schultz surrendered the CEO post, remaining only as chairman.

When Schultz gave up the day-to-day reins, there was sufficient deterioration in the corporate culture for him to eventually decide to return to full-time management as CEO. The importance of culture became not only even more evident to Schultz, but I believe to the market more broadly.

As I have amply discussed, the short-term focus inherent in the culture of many large financial services firms, particularly on the sell-side, is one of their main cultural problems. I discussed earlier how shareholder activists are often also blamed for prioritizing the short term. As I wrote then, one should be careful not to paint all shareholder activists with the same brush, as some do pressure company managements and boards to be more long-term oriented.

In his seminal book *Good to Great*, Jim Collins puts it the following way. "...boards at corporations should distinguish between share *value* and share *price*. Boards have no responsibility to a large chunk of the people who own company shares at any given moment, namely the share*flippers;* they should refocus their energies on creating great companies that build value for the share*holders.*

For a superb look at the board's role in taking a company from good to great, I recommend the book *Resisting Hostile Takeovers* by Rita Ricardo-Campbell (Praeger Publishers, 1997). Ms. Ricardo-Campbell was a Gillette board member during the Colman Mockler era and provides a detailed account of how a responsible board wrestled with the difficult and complex question of price versus value."

## Finally, a case study still in progress

Whole Foods Market (WFM), another company with a general reputation for a solid culture, is undergoing a transition in some ways reminiscent of what Starbucks went through prompting Schultz to return as CEO. In my opinion, how the company's stock performs from here on out will depend on how Whole Foods manages its current apparent cultural inflection point.

On paper, and based on the way Whole Foods' culture came across to outside observers for many years, all is well with its corporate DNA. The key question is whether the core of Whole Foods' culture is truly intact, despite the recent (hopefully for them, short-term) missteps.

In 2015 the company with a traditionally solid reputation faced an unusually high level of controversy. Whole Foods saw its short-term results suffer, and announced arguably adverse changes in employee compensation policies at roughly the same time as it faced investigations and lawsuits for 'mis-weighing errors'.

The 'weighing' scandal essentially entailed not quite giving consumers what they paid for. WFM still commands a certain valuation premium. Whether this remains, let alone expands back to the levels of its 'glory days', will (in my view) hinge upon whether the historically unique Whole Foods culture remains healthy at its core.

Following, from the company's own website, are some of the key features of Whole Foods' DNA as they are on the record (and at least used to be historically espoused by many of its employees).

OUR VALUES AND MISSION

Our motto—*Whole Foods, Whole People, Whole Planet* — emphasizes that our vision reaches beyond food retailing. In fact, our deepest purpose as an organization is helping support the health, well-being, and healing of both people — customers, Team Members, and business organizations in general — and the planet.

And our Core Values are not just words on a wall somewhere: they're guiding principles that inform every decision we make—from the daily, face-to-face interactions with our customers to larger decisions that impact the way Whole Foods Market evolves and grows.

We encourage our Team Members to connect with our Core Values on a personal level, choosing the one(s) that are most meaningful to them and making them "come to life" in their work. It is empowerment in its truest sense, and we think it's what can make working at Whole Foods Market such a unique and rewarding experience.

Our Core Values

- Selling the highest quality natural and organic products available

- Satisfying, delighting and nourishing our customers

- Supporting Team Member happiness and excellence

- Creating wealth through profits and growth

- Serving and supporting our local and global communities

- Practicing and advancing our environmental stewardship

- Creating ongoing win-win partnerships with our suppliers

- Promoting the health of our stakeholders through healthy eating education

Our Mission in Action

Since opening our first store in Austin, Texas in 1980, our whole business has been about making a difference – in the lives of our Team Members and the customers we serve, and in the communities and environments in which we operate.

What follows are just a few of the ways that Whole Foods Market's company culture reflects and reinforces our belief that companies should operate with a higher purpose beyond profits, and create value for all involved:

- We hold a regular, company-wide vote that allows Team Members to choose the health and benefits package they want the company to offer.

- 93% of stock options awarded since our IPO have gone to non-executive Team Members.

- A salary cap limits cash compensation (wages plus bonuses) to 19 times the average of all full-time Team Members employed during the year.

- Our financial books are open to Team Members, including our annual individual compensation report listing gross pay for all Team Members – even executives.

- Our Whole Planet Foundation is a not-for-profit group charged with combating poverty and promoting self-sufficiency in third-world countries that supply us with some of the products we sell.

- We have established a Global Team Member Emergency Fund for the benefit of Team Members throughout the company who become affected by major disasters such as hurricanes, tornadoes and wildfires.
- Our new Whole Cities Foundation is dedicated to supporting efforts that bring fresh, nutritious food and broader access to healthy eating education to underserved communities. It aims to build collaborative partnerships with community organizations that are poised to make significant impact in their neighborhoods to help improve individual and overall community health and wellness in the U.S.
- We regularly donate food and other products to support organizations such as homeless shelters, food banks, schools and others.
- Our Whole Trade program helps make it easy for customers to shop with conscience while bringing our commitment to transparent, ethical, and responsible sourcing and production to life. Whole Trade products must meet our high quality standards, provide more money to producers, ensure better wages and working conditions for workers, and promote a sustainable environment.
- We support local growers and vendors by providing a marketplace for their goods and doing what we can to contribute to the success of these growers and the local economy. Our Locally Grown initiative

creates local jobs and ensures the continuation of independent farming and the diversity of land use.

- Established in 2006, our Local Producer Loan Program provides up to $25 million in low-interest loans to independent local farmers and food artisans to help them expand their businesses.
- We are in the process of converting our distribution fleets to bio-diesel. Our goal is to move toward non-GMO bio-diesel as it becomes available.
- As part of our Green Mission, we promote environmentally sound practices for every aspect of store, facility and office operations.
- We purchase renewable energy credits (RECs) to offset 100% of the electricity used in all of our locations (retail and non-retail) in North America. In fact, Whole Foods Market ranked #2 on the list of America's top 20 purchasers of green power, according to the Environmental Protection Agency's (EPA) July 2013 Green Power Partnership report.
- Our Whole Kids Foundation's mission is to support schools and inspire families to improve children's nutrition and wellness. The foundation's ultimate goal is to get kids eating more veggies and fruits — and enjoying it!

## Conclusion

It is intriguing how prevalent the concept of 'delighting' customers, users, guests, clients or whatever term is used for the firm's consumers among companies with excellent cultures. Therefore, in evaluating the quality of a company's DNA, one of the first characteristics to look at is its focus on the consumer. Whether delighting its customers is a true and widespread commitment at all levels of an organization tells you a lot about its long-term prospects.

If a company is committed to not only serving but truly delighting its customers, then the overwhelming chances are that it is also determined to treat its employees with respect and dignity, as in the case of Starbucks. Only employees that see a purpose in their jobs, that broadly share the core values of their company, are likely to go out of their way to please their customers.

Employees that are treated well are more likely to treat the consumer well. This contributes to a virtuous cycle in which all of a company's stakeholders can thrive. In the long run, which is what really matters, the interests of all stakeholders tend to converge.

A long-term orientation is not only best for shareholders, but a company's employees and customers also benefit. A long-term oriented management is less likely to treat employees unfairly or implement layoffs at the first signs of a temporary drop in demand in order to try to make its quarterly or even annual earnings guidance.

Likewise, a corporation's customers benefit from a true long-term orientation, as the company is less likely to cut corners in order to make its short-term numbers. It is paramount to the long-term success of a corporation to enjoy customer trust.

Customer trust is indeed one of the key cultural features of both Starbucks and Apple, among the most valuable brands in the world (as well as arguably among the most successful large companies of all time). Apple, according to TIME the most respected company in the world, recently demonstrated the utmost importance to it of customer trust.

In a controversial decision, the company's CEO Tim Cook refused to comply with the FBI-requested court order to have Apple effectively write code that would break the iPhone's encryption. Much was written both supporting and criticizing Apple's response to the FBI's publicly disseminated request, but the company's decision is very much in line with its historical stance on the privacy of its customers.

This brings us to an important point. It is not necessarily the specific values that are the hallmark of a company's corporate culture that make it a good or bad one. Since such a qualification is highly subjective, what really matters are the consistency and durability of those characteristics.

It is very important to employees to know what to expect and to have clear guidelines on how they should operate in the long run. Strong corporate cultures typically entail the relevant company's employees knowing how to handle controversial situations by referring to the key values embedded in the company's culture. Alphabet, for example, has not changed its mission, which sets it apart, and is another key cultural trait. When challenged at the time, Google decided to exit the key Chinese market rather than compromise its values.

Employees who act consistently according to a well-understood set of corporate beliefs have a better chance to contribute to a customer experience that reinforces the customer's trust in the company. In a sort of virtuous cycle, employees who operate in a positive corporate cultural environment consistently act in a way that reinforces that corporate culture and that creates a consistently positive customer experience, which over time builds and maintains customer trust.

*Corporate governance – Much room to improve...globally*

As the key thesis for this book, I have argued that corporate culture is an under-researched area in investment research. Corporate *governance* issues are a little better understood, researched and discussed, but still generally not well enough, in my view.

As I have endeavored to explain, there is much confusion and misunderstanding. Many observers seem to think that the better the corporate governance in a company, the more likely the short-term thinking and acting on the part of management! Nothing could be further from the truth.

While there are companies that exemplify a long-term vision while at the same time displaying poor corporate governance (Google and Facebook, for instance), there are many more companies with sound corporate governance practices *and* a long-term vision.

Again, long-term thinking and excellent corporate governance are by no means mutually exclusive. Don't let anyone (not even my *beloved* Alphabet) tell you otherwise! Although corporate governance is obviously not the same as corporate culture, I view the former as a subcomponent of the latter. In the specific case of Google, I think its corporate culture is *excellent overall,* despite the fact that I consider the company's corporate governance to be somewhat flawed.

Since I will leave a more detailed discussion of the subcomponent of culture that is corporate governance for another day (perhaps a subsequent book), suffice it to say here that I believe that the closer the corporate governance aligns with the overall culture of the company, the better the long-term results, everything else being equal.

I heard Hewlett Packard Enterprise's CEO Meg Whitman say once that "boards have cultures too." The board of directors of a company, by virtue of its size (a rough average of nine people), has certain group dynamics and a culture of its own. Ideally, the board of directors has a culture that aligns well with that of the overall company.

The board of directors is the entity through which a company's shareholders hold management accountable. Let us again remember that a publicly listed corporation belongs to all of its shareholders. Ideally, one share entitles shareholders to one vote in key corporate matters, such as the election of directors to compose the board. Here is where the Alphabet and Facebook corporate governance practices present key flaws.

The company's CEO (even if he or she also happens to be the company's founder) reports to the shareholders through the board of directors. Thus, in my view, ideally the CEO is not at the same time the chairman of the board of directors. A separation of those key titles aimed at reducing the potential for conflicts of interest indicates better corporate governance, everything else being equal. Board representation of a meaningful number of independent directors (those not employed by the company or otherwise closely aligned with management) is also indicative of better corporate governance.

I elected not to make corporate governance a key topic of this book. As I previously noted, I believe corporate governance is better understood than corporate culture. Nonetheless, I would like to add that there is a general misperception regarding how emerging markets stack up in terms of corporate governance practices (and, consequently, the protections of the rights of minority shareholders) when compared to the more developed countries. For instance, when Alibaba (BABA) chose to list its shares in the US, the financial media often attributed the decision largely to the depth of the US financial markets.

It is true that the US has very deep and liquid markets. Nevertheless, Hong Kong, where Alibaba was originally expected to list its stock, refused to agree to the dual-class share structure that the company chose. Therefore, the more forgiving US market regulations when it comes to the ability for companies to list non-voting stock (or equity with more limited voting rights than what the controlling shareholders own) was in fact a key reason behind BABA listing here. In reality, the US is allowing poorer corporate governance practices than Hong Kong! Companies can choose where to list their stock (or alternatively, where to incorporate) in order to pursue certain corporate governance practices.

### Afterword

The prevalence of short-term oriented corporate cultures across Wall Street has been responsible for what some call the 'financialization' of the economy at large. To the extent that the financial industry has pushed a culture of short-termism on to other industries and around the world, excessive financialization is certainly a negative. I have always believed that anything, when taken to an excessive level, can become a bad thing; extreme positions are always dangerous.

There are growing calls for financial penetration in the economy (the share of finance as a percentage of GDP) to return to some lower level it once had in the US. This oversimplifies too complex an issue. Yet, I am also not advocating an ever-larger financial penetration as the way forward. This is probably an area not to be explicitly *targeted* through legislation or regulation.

Deceptive practices, abuses and the like should be penalized, in some cases with meaningful prison terms. But unethical behavior can and does take place in countries with high financial penetration (such as the US), *as well* as in those where financial services represent a very low share of the national GDP. Therefore, it is not financialization per se, but #shortermism that is at the root of the problem (our real global nemesis).

The world, led by the US, has gone too far on the path of globalization to even attempt to reverse course now. Calls for nationalism (and away from globalization) entail simplistic approaches to what are complicated, long-term problems. Reversing course now would represent just another short-term fix, simply in the opposite direction. Too many people in the negatively affected regions and segments of society have suffered too much already for their sacrifice to have been in vain.

Needless to say, I believe that free-market capitalism in an increasingly globalized economy is the right long-term approach to many of the world's problems. The first step towards a more democratic shareholder capitalism entails not reversing course, but fixing what is wrong with our system, for the long haul.

In her recent book *Makers and Takers,* Time's assistant managing editor and economics columnist Rana Foroohar powerfully explains and criticizes the pervasive nature of financialization in our society. She comes up with a set of broad prescriptions to deal with it in order to 'save capitalism'. While the book is very well researched and written, I disagree with many of Ms. Foroohar's key conclusions.

For starters, I think that she misdiagnoses the problem, considering it to be financialization itself. As I have noted, I believe pervasive short-termism is really the root cause, and financialization merely a large symptom of it. Ms. Foroohar's book was published at the time I was putting the finishing touches on my own publication. Thus, only in this afterword will I address some of my concerns stemming from *Makers and Takers*, although there is much on which I do agree with Ms. Foroohar's analysis.

As I have extensively written in the past, I think that a *balanced* approach towards research and development (R&D), capital expenditures, dividends and stock buybacks is the ideal. Corporate boards and managements should never yield to short-term pressures (from Wall Street or anybody else). Their focus and their obligation are towards the long-term success of their corporations. This entails balancing the needs and demands of all stakeholders, but again, with a focus always on the long run.

Ms. Foroohar takes on Apple (AAPL) as a key example of financialization and financial engineering at work. She criticizes this great company for no longer investing sufficiently in innovation. I believe nothing could be further from the truth. While Apple's R&D *as a percent of revenues* have indeed declined, the absolute dollars invested in research and development at AAPL have continued to increase quite sharply.

Much having to do with 'the law of large numbers' applies to Apple, and this is also the case when it comes to R&D. Continuing to increase R&D (or even keeping it flat) as a percent of significantly increasing sales over the long run would probably be irresponsible. Trees cannot grow to the sky. The same goes for capital expenditures. There should be some efficiencies from ever-growing scale. Therefore, it is absolutely warranted for Apple to return some of its excess cash to shareholders, as it is currently doing.

IBM has been widely criticized (more deservedly, in my view) for financial engineering. One of the poster children for share repurchases, IBM has more of a long-running practice of shrinking its outstanding share base through aggressive stock buybacks funded by increasing net debt. Critics, including Ms. Foroohar, take the criticism too far and condemn the practice of share repurchases too broadly. Nonetheless, I also do not accept that aggressive stock buybacks are always good, and I do agree that they are sometimes (though definitely not always) used as financial engineering.

It is a fact that cutting the count of shares outstanding, through spreading any given level of earnings over a smaller number of shares, has the effect of boosting EPS, everything else being equal. Thus, the practice can theoretically be abused by short-term focused management being particularly aggressive during a quarter of poor financial performance in order to show better EPS trends than otherwise would be the case.

But not all share repurchases are created equal. There is nothing wrong with stock buybacks as a consistent way to distribute *part* of the total remuneration to shareholders. It is very important that the actual number of shares outstanding does consistently drop when a company has a practice of meaningful stock buybacks. Many companies use stock as an important component of their executive compensation. There is also nothing wrong with this practice in and of itself. Aligning the interests of management with that of shareholders is actually a positive, provided that the programs focus on *long-term* performance.

In fact, I would advocate extending shareholder ownership programs to *all* levels of employees in an organization, and even to a company's customers, freelance associates and suppliers. It is in the interest of all parties involved for as many as possible consumers to be more knowingly and actively involved in the ownership of corporations.

Therefore, in 2015 I filed for a patent for what I call the "consume-to-invest" (c2i) stock ownership program. According to this idea, consumers would be offered company stock instead of cash discounts through price cuts and promotions. Establishing such a practice would not only generate increased consumer loyalty but a sense of ownership in the corporation that would be a key first step towards reducing the gap (and potential resentment) of individual consumers vs. the owners of capital.

The c2i program could easily be expanded to existing corporate loyalty and reward programs. Moreover, with the possibility of owning shares in a client, the program could be extended also to a corporation's suppliers. As our economy continues to evolve and the labor marketplace consists increasingly of freelance workers, the corporate shareholder ownership program could easily be expanded to include such participants in the 'gig' economy. Instead of receiving all of their compensation from multiple 'employers' in cash, freelancers could choose to get *some* of their pay in stock of one of the companies for which they work.

I obviously believe that sharing the success with employees at all levels in the organization is good management, good policy, part of a good culture (and creates economic value in the long run). However, if a corporation uses large dilutive issues of stock to compensate its management and employees, it must also buy back a significant amount of shares in the market just to keep its total share count from increasing. All this highlights that the topic is a lot more complex than Ms. Foroohar and other critics argue. In my opinion, broader participation in the equity market (as long as it is with a long-term focus) can only be seen as a positive.

Finally on the topic of share buybacks, it is very important that a company uses only *excess* cash generation to repurchase stock in the long haul. Increasingly, as Ms. Foroohar notes, corporations are issuing debt to finance large share buybacks. To the extent there is a significant increase in *net* debt as a result of stock repurchases, it is definitely a red flag for financial engineering.

This brings us to the issue of financial leverage. Like with anything else, the use of leverage, to an excessive level, is a negative. Nevertheless, the use of financial leverage in and of itself is not a negative. *Prudent* use of leverage, everything else being equal, does contribute to greater economic activity.

A closer alignment in the interests of various stakeholders at the corporate level in our free-market capitalist system (which in recent decades has been increasingly embraced around the world) would continue to improve its long-term prospects.

To the extent that growing numbers of would-be small investors participate in the long-term rewards of stock ownership, they will be increasingly vested in the success of an ever-larger number of corporations. The c2i concept is a simple first step to address the growing socio-economic polarization due to the gap between those who own capital and those who do not.

My proposed approach, as opposed to Ms. Foroohar's, is not to deliberately shrink the size of the financial sector. Instead, *more* economic agents (including the average person on the street) should more *knowingly* participate in the ownership of corporations. In a way, through disintermediation, this will likely result in a loss of clout for the conventional financial industry.

Still, stock ownership is unequivocally *not* a negative. Where I do agree with Ms. Foroohar is in that debt should not be favored by the US tax code. More broadly, as do many politicians on both sides of the aisle, I strongly believe that our byzantine tax code should be simplified; tax reform is increasingly urgent.

Despite my calls for a more simplified tax code, I agree with Ms. Foroohar that capital gains tax rates should be further differentiated to encourage more long-term thinking. Currently, the tax rules essentially define one year as sufficient to qualify for long-term treatment. Perhaps the lower capital gains tax should only kick in for assets held for two years or more.

Another approach could be to have a sliding tax rate with each full year (with a minimum of two to qualify as long term). Well beyond the scope of this book, and amply covered by many others, is the need to harmonize US corporate taxes with practices elsewhere in the developed world. Many experts have advocated the introduction to the US of a territorial tax system, with a one-time lower (say 10%) tax rate granted to corporate cash brought back from overseas.

Contrary to Ms. Foroohar, I think that broader ownership of company shares should be encouraged (even by the tax code). The specific focus of this book has not been the virtues of equity investing. There are many great books on the subject. Suffice it to reiterate here my strong belief that long-term ownership of stocks is one of the best paths to wealth *for all*. Even people who disagree with this assertion probably would concur that we do need more financial literacy. Ms. Foroohar may disagree with this notion, but her book argues that what she calls financialization has been at work for many decades. This includes a period in which the American economy was thriving by most accounts.

I do not believe that the legacy of a more involved public in the ownership of corporations is a bad trend that should be reversed. To the contrary, broader ownership of stocks may lead to my ideal of a more inclusive, socially conscious corporate ownership democracy.

One of the most important lessons when it comes to this is that only money that savers (prospective investors) consider for the stock market should be funds that will *not* be needed in the short term. I always advocate a time horizon of no less than five years for investments in the equity market. Fighting short-termism is thus a key tenet of improving financial literacy.

Focusing on the very long term, James Fletcher founded the non-profit Young Investors Society (yis.org). We are teaching high school kids to be long-term investors. When asked to provide a key piece of advice for young people, I came up with the following. First of all: money is not everything. Certainly, money does not buy happiness, although many of people's major worries do tend to center around money issues. Once you have enough financial resources to cover your basic needs, however, money makes less of a difference to people's well-being than most believe. At the time our life in this world ends, we are all truly equal. We cannot take anything with us.

This realization leads me to two separate conclusions. The first one applies to how I try to live my life *other than when it comes to money.* I try to live each day as if it was my last. I try to enjoy the present and focus on the short term. My second conclusion then has to do with money. When it comes to financial matters, I try to be as long-term oriented as my risk tolerance will allow. *Other than to cover my family's basic needs,* money plays no role in the short term.

Money is for the very long term, hopefully for being able to give back. So here is my heartfelt advice. Try to keep your short-term financial needs to a minimum. Live modestly, and enjoy the great things in life that are free, always treasuring the moment. Try to live each day as if it were your last; you never know. It might just be. On financial matters, save as much as you can for the future. Pay not only your likely future self, but invest for the long term, when the wealth you create can help shape a better world for your children and your children's children.

Additionally, in the end, we are *all* investors. We may think our own financial decisions might not be important enough to qualify us as investors. Still, how we choose to spend our *time,* automatically makes us investors, if not of money, of time. I do not necessarily agree with the notion that time is money, as that gives money more importance than it deserves. Time, when it comes to us as individuals, is finite and arguably the most precious of all 'non-renewable' resources available to us. How we invest our time has most important repercussions in the long-term course of our lives and that of those we love.

If you agree with me that we are *all* investors, the question is how good we are at it. We should all strive to become ever better investors, investors in companies, investors in our communities and investors in ourselves. All the profits from this book will go to Young Investors Society (YIS). Having purchased it, thus, you are starting to do your part. Please continue to be involved. Go to yis.org to donate a bit more, if you can. Get involved in your community. If you are already part of YIS, spread the word. If you happen to be a high school kid not on YIS, launch a chapter at your school. And yet once more (since this is my key take-away), let us all strive to become ever better *long-term* investors. Let's bring an end to #shortermism.